The Boys of the Dark

ALSO BY ROBIN GABY FISHER

After the Fire

The BOYS OF THE DARK

A Story of Betrayal and Redemption in the Deep South

ROBIN GABY FISHER

with MICHAEL O'McCARTHY
and ROBERT W. STRALEY

ST. MARTIN'S PRESS
NEW YORK

www.stmartins.com

Library of Congress Cataloging-in-Publication Data

Fisher, Robin Gaby.
    The boys of the dark : a story of betrayal and redemption in the deep south / Robin Gaby Fisher ; with Michael O'McCarthy and Robert W. Straley. — 1st ed.
        p.   cm.
    ISBN 978-1-250-03925-5
    1. Florida School for Boys—History.   2. Reformatories—Florida—History.   3. Imprisonment—Florida—History.
4. Abused children—Florida—History.   I. O'McCarthy, Michael.   II. Straley, Robert W.   III. Title.
    HV9105.F72.F554   2010
    365'.42—dc22   2009045734

First Edition: August 2010

10   9   8   7   6   5   4   3   2   1

Events as recounted in the following pages are the basis of a civil action in which many of the people telling their stories herein are plaintiffs. Their stories remain under investigation and none of the alleged perpetrators of the torture and abuses they claim to have suffered have been charged or convicted of a crime.

The Boys of the Dark

CHAPTER ONE

It was the touch of a stranger's hand that shook him free from his murderous thoughts. Before the soft, plump hand intervened, he'd been walking through the Super Kmart looking for, of all things, a battery charger.

Out of the blue, chilling images of brutality and violence began whirling in his head like frames on a spinning reel of film. Apparently he was muttering profanities, too, because, as he was coming out of that familiar dark void, he recognized the sound of his own angry voice.

Startled, he looked first down at his hands—they were balled into fists—and then into the face of a stranger.

The woman was middle-aged with sallow skin and dull, brown hair, spun with threads of gray. Her turned-down mouth gave her an air of sternness, but her eyes were soft and kind and she looked genuinely concerned.

"You all right, fella?" she asked.

Robert's face was splotched red with embarrassment. People were gathered and he could hear their murmurs.

The guy's crazy.

Is he alone?

Someone had better call security.

He locked eyes with the woman and held her probing gaze until he felt steady enough to move.

Perspiration dripped from his forehead and stung his eyes. When, he wondered, did his thinking turn from charging the dead battery in his van to revenge on some faceless adversary? He wasn't sure.

But then Robert never knew when he was about to go into one of his trances, or why he had such wretched thoughts.

As an adolescent, Robert thought a demon was in him. For a long time he reassured himself that his evil fantasies would one day subside, yet the intervening decades had not brought peace of mind; indeed, the uncontrolled episodes had intensified and come more frequent with age.

This one was so public and so obvious that he caused a scene in the store. He was frightened and ashamed.

"Can I call someone?" the woman asked.

"I'm sorry," Robert stuttered, his mouth twisting into a grimace.

"Are you okay?" she asked.

"I'm all right," he said, turning and walking quickly toward the exit. "Sometimes I just . . . I'm all right now."

Robert was not all right. He was nearly sixty years old and could not remember the last time he felt all right.

His hard luck began, he thought, when he was born, by cesarean section, to a mother who was prone to her own fits of rage. His mother was a piece of work, all right. She used to tell him stories about her days as a chorus girl and, over his pleas and protestations, insisted he learn tap dancing, saying his "girlie legs" were pretty enough to carry him all the way to a chorus line some day. She had said it so many times when he was small, Robert later told people, "It's a wonder I didn't grow up to be a flaming queen."

Robert grew up on a tiny lake in rural central Florida. His parents had built their cinder-block house piecemeal, and although it never seemed whole, what was there was pristine and generously shaded by palmetto palm and oak trees. Rattlesnakes and sinkholes posed the biggest threat to the harmony of everyday life for most of the folks who lived on the lake. Robert had his mother to contend with. At least his father could get away.

Robert's father was a burly man who could hold his own in a bar fight, but at home he was subject to the strict rules of his overbearing wife, and he always ceded to her. Raymond Straley looked like Roy Rogers, but with one eye. He had lost the other eye in 1945 when his tank was bombed during the Battle of Okinawa. As a younger man, he ran moonshine in West Virginia, but by the time Robert was old enough to know better, Raymond was making a legal living, hauling sides of beef for the Lykes Brothers Cattle Company in Tampa. He told Robert that he couldn't explain it, but he loved the road more than almost anything else in his life. He worked more than he was home. It didn't take much for Robert to figure out that the job was his father's way of escaping from the captivity of his stifling marriage. Robert didn't blame his father. He went to bed most nights wishing he could get away from his mother, too.

If only he had known then what would happen once he got his wish.

Robert's mother was certainly peculiar. A shapely, raven-haired beauty, she fancied herself an entertainer. More than anything else, she told her little boy, she had wanted to be an actress, and even changed her name from Betty to Elisa because it sounded more dramatic. Her unexpected pregnancy had foiled her dreams of celebrity, though, and she seemed never to have gotten over it. "This is what kids do for you," she used to tell Robert, lifting her blouse to expose the ropelike cesarean scar that spanned her middle.

Between cleaning compulsively and hounding her submissive husband, when he was home, and her diminutive only child, who was at her beck and call, Robert's mother spent her days composing songs and writing plays. Robert's role was to memorize the lyrics and scripts and perform them at her whim. Even though it made him feel like the sissy his classmates at Lake Magdalene Elementary School accused him of being, compliance was still easier than making a fuss and triggering his mother's temper.

If Robert and his friends had any doubts as to whether the Straleys were the oddest family in their North Tampa community, they were erased the first time Robert invited a group of neighborhood kids to the house and his mother performed for them, singing and playing her bongo drums. By the following morning, everyone at school had heard about the impromptu recital, and Robert was a laughingstock. He was ten years old and never brought another friend home after that.

As entertaining as Robert's mother could be, her moods swung wildly, and her wrath was fierce. He never knew what might set her off. A moved tchotchke on a shelf or a footprint on a freshly swept rug was all it took. Then there was hell to pay.

The emotional mauling was agonizing, and Robert used to wish she would smack him rather than badger him relentlessly for days after some perceived transgression.

Robert had not yet experienced the excruciating pain of physical torture.

When Robert's mother's mood darkened, her eyes turned black and her mouth frothed as she spewed her hatred until his ears actually ached. As much as her angry words hurt him, it was her surreptitious attacks, the ones she had clearly planned and he never saw coming, that were most disturbing to him. When she invited Robert to watch a movie on television that he was dying to see, he couldn't believe his good fortune. Then, just before the climax, she switched off the set and walked away with a satisfied grin. He went to bed and cried himself to sleep.

Even when Robert asked her, "Mother, what have I done to make you hate me so much?" she never backed down or comforted him or said she was sorry. Her seeming lack of remorse over anything she did had served her well at least once.

One of Robert's early memories is of his mother shaking him awake in the middle of the night to say an intruder was trying to break into the house. She was as cool as a cucumber. "Don't make any noise," she said, aiming her .38-caliber police special at the front door. Robert heard the door squeak open and then what sounded like a cannon exploding in his ear. He looked up just in time to see the silhouette of a black man falling backward out of the door. His mother pulled the door in, tied it shut with a piece of clothesline, and went back to bed. The next morning, the police found the man dead on the side of a road near their house. When they came to the door to question Robert's mother, she explained that the stranger had tried to break in, in the middle of the night, so she shot him. The case was closed and his mother never mentioned the incident again.

It wasn't long afterward that Robert started running away. The police always found him and brought him back home. The last time, when Robert was thirteen, he hooked up with two boys who were joyriding in a car they had taken from a relative. One of the boys had decided that running away to Miami Beach to be beach bums sounded like a good idea, but they didn't even make it out of Tampa before they were caught.

That time, when the police brought Robert home, his mother refused to take him back.

"I don't care what you do with him," she had told the officers. "But he's not coming back here. I don't want him."

As a minor, with a history of running away, Robert was shipped off to reform school. There he would learn what evil really was. That was the beginning of a long descent into a madness from which he had never recovered.

Robert stewed about the scene in Kmart for days after it happened, in that fall of 2006. The spell had been his worst yet and he was afraid to leave the house for fear of another public humiliation. *Maybe,* he thought, *the trance had been brought on by exhaustion from spending so many weeks on the road.* Robert had only been back home in Clearwater for two days when the battery in his van died and he went shopping for the charger. Before that, he had been working twenty-hour days, and when he wasn't working, he was driving, sometimes as much as eight hundred miles in a day to get to his next show.

As unlucky as Robert had been in so many areas of his life, he was fortunate in business. After his marriage ended in 1993, when his wife Teresa had told him, "I love you, Robert, but you have so many dark corners," he spent almost all of his time building up the company he founded twenty years earlier. Robert sold carnival novelties for a living. It wasn't the most romantic career, but it provided him with a more than comfortable living and an escape from his loveless life. Glow sticks and flashing necklaces were all the rage at festivals from Little Rock to Oshkosh to Oswego, and Robert cashed in on them big time. The cheap trinkets had paid for houses in two states, exotic vacations, and pretty much anything else that caught his eye. One show could easily reap ten thousand dollars, but the kind of cash that Robert made required spending the entire summer on the road, traveling the national festival circuit.

Tour schedules were punishing, with seven-day workweeks and days that began at sunup and ended well past midnight in cheap motels. Sometimes Robert lost track of which city he was in until it was time to pack up the van and map a route to the next festival. Each stop meant unloading a truckload of merchandise, interviewing and hiring a crew to sell the goods, job training—*Don't be afraid to sell. Don't stand in front of a booth. Don't block the sidewalks. Seven-hour shifts. No breaks. No alcoholic beverages. No absconding with the profits.* The standard was three to eight days in a city, and then the process began all over again. Even a young man would be challenged by the work Robert did. The last tour had lasted nearly six months and seemed especially grueling, perhaps, he thought, because his age was finally catching up with him.

If he wanted to avoid another humiliating scene like the one in Kmart, he needed to take it easy for a while.

Six weeks passed before Robert could go a day without dwelling on the dreadful incident. Fall had given way to winter.

Florida's early December sky was the color of blue lapis, and a clean breeze blew off the Gulf of Mexico.

Sitting at his kitchen table, Robert scanned the morning newspaper. As he buttered his toast, his attention was drawn to a photograph of a boy whose eyes sparkled with the innocence of youth. He stared at the picture for a long time.

It was the oddest feeling. Something drew him in, he wasn't sure what, but he felt as if he was looking at a picture of himself at a young age.

Emotion choked in Robert's throat and tears spilled down his cheeks. Bewildered, he wiped his face, thinking that it felt odd to cry. The last time he did was probably ten years earlier, when he learned that his daughter, his only child, with whom he had reconciled after a long estrangement, had taken her own life. Before that, he didn't know.

The story in the *Miami Herald* said the boy in the picture died at a Florida boot camp the previous January. The local sheriff claimed that fourteen-year-old Martin Lee Anderson collapsed and died during a mandatory run. But a surveillance film showed a team of drill instructors pushing the boy to keep running after he collapsed in the dirt. When he didn't obey their orders, the men piled on top of him, and one covered his mouth with a cloth until his writhing body went limp. It had taken the state months to charge the guards, but the case against them was finally headed to trial.

"Tinged with racial overtones and the clash of cultures as new Florida meets old, the trial of seven boot camp guards and a nurse in the death of fourteen-year-old Martin Lee Anderson will be watched throughout the nation," the *Herald* wrote.

"The likelihood of conviction, some observers say, may be dim in this close-knit, God-fearing, law-and-order community where residents are more likely to speak with a drawl than an accent.

"'That prosecutor has one heck of a job on his hands,' said Miami lawyer Edward Carhart, a former chief Miami-Dade prosecutor who defended a police officer charged with covering up the death of Miami motorcyclist Arthur McDuffie. 'If he has to try these people in the Panhandle, I give the odds as 10-1 against him.'"

Robert finished reading and felt that terrible, black curtain fall over his consciousness, and the rage begin to seethe inside him.

For a long time, he sat trancelike with the newspaper spread out in front of him.

The sound of the silence was broken when his clenched fist slammed the table.

CHAPTER TWO

R obert jolted up in his bed. His heart was jackhammering through his pajama top. The same nightmare had robbed him of sleep hundreds of times over the years.

He was a boy again, walking into a shadowy pit. A pair of malevolent eyes pierced the darkness, yet despite the leg-rattling terror he felt, he could not stop himself from moving forward. The owner of the eyes, a creature with malformed limbs, slithered toward him. He believed that if he looked into the eyes of the beast he would go insane. That was when he woke up.

But something was different this time. Trembling, Robert realized that the tragedy of Martin Lee Anderson, the boy killed at the Florida boot camp, had ignited in him something he had denied his whole life—a time of such depravity and evil that, when it was over, he locked his memories away in a box and threw away the key. The past has a way of stealing into the present, though, and he could no longer elude that terrible truth from long ago. Robert was staring into the face of the monster.

He curled onto his side and his mind forced him back forty-three years.

Bobby Straley watched the green blur of poplar and pine rush by as the rickety bus hurdled toward the Florida School for Boys.

The year was 1963; the month, March. The trip from Tampa, north to Marianna, had taken most of the day. Bobby had grown more leery with each mile. He was barely thirteen, and the only other times he had been away from home were occasional trips to his grandmother's house—and the times he ran away, of course, but that was only for a night or two. Running away was what got him into this predicament.

When the judge sentenced Bobby to a year in reform school, then pounded the gavel with such force that Bobby jumped in his seat, he decided he would run again rather than be locked up with a bunch of hoodlums. But he hadn't had the chance to get away, not with his hands and feet bound with chains and beefy guards at each elbow.

Bobby was terrified when the journey to Marianna began. The four other boys on the bus were bigger and stronger-looking and even they looked scared. How would a puny kid like him survive? Small and timid as he was, he'd be ripe for the picking by the bullies on campus, and from what he'd heard, there were plenty of bullies in reform school. Bobby had never even been in a fight.

By the time the bus maneuvered the long, winding lane from the road to the reformatory, Bobby felt his shoulders, which for most of the trip had been up around his ears, finally begin to relax. The school grounds were picturesque. Bobby took in the manicured lawns and trimmed hedges, the red-clay basketball courts, and the cozy-looking cottages and wondered, "How bad can it be here?"

The bus grinded to a stop outside a large brick building and a tall, sober-looking man boarded and ordered the boys out. He led them into the building, to a tiny office on the first floor. The unsmiling but not unpleasant-seeming man watched as a guard, called a houseman, unlocked the chains on Bobby's ankles, then his wrists. The chains clanked on the cement floor. Bobby was measured and weighed. The scale read 105 pounds. The other boys snickered and the tall man glared at them. State-issued uniforms and shoes were handed to the five newcomers and, after a short indoctrination speech, they were escorted to their living quarters.

Bobby was taken to the Lincoln Cottage, which housed boys his age. The cottage was inviting, with a large reading parlor at one end and a Ping-Pong table at the other. A long hallway led to the dormitory, a spotless white room with three rows of army cots, ten cots in each row spaced about two feet apart. Bobby's escort assigned him a cot and said to report to the mess hall for dinner in an hour sharp. "Yessir," Bobby said.

When the escort left, Bobby quickly changed into his reform school uniform and drifted outside, hoping to find a friend. He sauntered toward a bench where three boys sat, talking. They didn't acknowledge him at first, and he was too shy to introduce himself. Bobby stood there awkwardly for a moment or two, long enough to hear that the boys were planning an escape. They didn't seem to mind that he was listening.

"Want to come with us?" one of the boys asked finally, looking at Bobby and tilting his head toward the way out.

"Uh-uh," Bobby said uncertainly. "I just got here. I think I'll stick it out for a while."

The boy who issued the invitation shrugged at the same moment the dinner gong sounded. Bobby followed the boys to the mess hall. He devoured a plate of beans and potatoes and returned to his cottage as instructed earlier by his escort. As he walked between the rows of cots, toward his assigned bunk, he noticed the three boys from the bench. He nodded knowingly toward one of the boys as he passed, but the boy seemed to look through him. The others didn't even look up as he passed. The cottage father, who lived upstairs and whose job it was to supervise the dorm, called roll. All thirty boys were present.

March nights in the Florida Panhandle are often chilly, and the dorm was so cold that Bobby could see his breath. He wondered how he would keep warm beneath the single thin blanket he had been issued. He curled himself into a ball, hoping to benefit from his own body heat.

"Lights out," someone shouted.

The dormitory went dark.

A moment later, the beam from a flashlight cut through the darkness of the dorm, illuminating the face of one of the boys from the bench. Bobby saw the silhouette of the tall man, the one who had greeted the bus earlier that day, standing over the boy.

"You!" the tall man barked at the wide-eyed boy. "Get up! Now!"

The flashlight swung right, to the face of a second boy from the bench.

"And you! Get up!"

Then the third boy.

"You, too! Up! Now!"

Bobby saw the light swerve his way. He quickly turned his face toward the wall and closed his eyes tightly. He sensed the tall man looming over him. A second that seemed like forever passed before he felt the man's hot breath on his cheek.

"Get up, you sissy!" the tall man said, spitting out his words with such scorn that his spittle rained on Bobby's face.

"Move!"

All four boys were led from the dorm to a waiting black sedan. They were dressed only in their school-issued white cotton undershorts. Bobby shivered uncontrollably, uncertain whether it was from the chill in the air or the pure fright he felt.

Standing beside the car was a short, barrel-chested man who glared at them through thick black-rimmed spectacles. The sinister-looking man had one arm, but he looked powerful. It was clear to Bobby, from the man's look of distain, that he and the other three boys might as well have been cockroaches or rats.

"You talk about running away, you're going down," said the one-armed man, grinning to reveal brown-stained teeth.

Bobby was too new to the reform school to know that the tall, lanky man was Robert W. Hatton, the school director and chief disciplinarian, and the squat man with one arm was a supervisor named Troy Tidwell. He didn't know what "going down" meant, either. But it sounded ominous, and he hadn't talked about running anyway, he had simply listened while the other boys planned their getaway. He needed to set things straight.

Tidwell ordered the boys into the backseat of the sedan. Bobby was last in line.

"I wasn't going to run," he said timidly, climbing unsteadily into the backseat of the car to join the three other boys.

The one-armed man yanked him back out with such brute

force that Bobby imagined his own scrawny arm snapping, like a dry twig. Panting, the man closed in on Bobby's face. His breath stank from what smelled like a combination of tobacco juice and, Bobby couldn't quite put his finger on it, something sickening sweet. He tried to hold his breath to keep from drawing in the man's putrid breath but he couldn't help it, he was so frightened he began to wheeze. That seemed to make the one-armed man even angrier, and he moved in closer.

"You don't speak unless you are spoken to, you hear me, boy?" Tidwell said, twisting Bobby's arm behind his back and shoving him into the backseat of the car.

Tidwell slid onto the seat next to Bobby and Hatton gunned the motor. The car lurched forward and, within what couldn't have been more than a minute or two, slowed to a stop in front of a small, white stucco building.

Hatton ordered the boys out of the car and led them into the building. A single, dim ceiling bulb shed an eerie light in the hallway and the air smelled foul. The boys were ordered to line up with their backs against the wall. The walls were damp and moldy. Hatton pointed a crooked finger at the first boy in line.

"This way," he said, his voice flat with indifference, leading the boy to an open door where Tidwell was waiting.

The men and the boy disappeared around the corner, and the door slammed behind them, but not before Hatton flipped a wall switch and a large industrial-type fan began to rumble. Bobby and the other boys shared sideways glances, although they didn't dare make eye contact for fear of what they might read in each other's expressions.

"Why am I here?" Bobby asked himself. "And what is happening behind that door?"

The roar of the fan did not completely drown out the noises coming from the other room. Thwacking sounds, as if from a sharp blow with a flat object, were followed by faint grunts, which quickly escalated into anguished, pitiful yowls, like the cries of a mortally wounded animal. Bobby wanted to cup his hands over his ears, so as not to hear, but he was too terrified to move.

When quiet finally came to pass, the door opened and the boy was shoved out. He was hunched over, his hands clenched together between his legs. His face was as white as chalk, his eyes were vacant, and saliva spilled from his gaping mouth. He was gasping, as if he has just seen the devil himself. Bobby looked from the boy's tear-stained face to the blood dripping down his spindly white legs. He wondered if the boy would die.

Hatton stepped forward and grabbed the next boy in line. The boy struggled and an older student, he was maybe seventeen, emerged from behind the door and shoved him toward Tidwell. Tidwell smirked. Bobby noticed that his glasses were crooked on his face. Hatton flipped the wall switch and again the fan whirred. The door banged shut, but Bobby could still hear the boy behind it whimpering.

Bobby's heart rattled and he considered running, but his legs felt like iron stumps, too heavy to move. Besides, where would he have gone? He held his ears, trying not to scream. But through his cupped hands he heard long, plaintive wails. His whole body shuddered.

After what seemed like forever, the door opened and the second boy stumbled out, landing at Bobby's feet. His back was covered with bleeding welts and his white undershorts were in shreds, stuck in the oozing skin of his buttocks.

When the door closed after the third boy, Bobby felt himself sliding down the damp wall. His legs could no longer hold him, and this time when the screams began, he wailed, too. He was seized by fear, his terror so acute that he hardly noticed when the noise behind the door finally stopped. A hand grabbed his arm.

"You're next," the tall man sneered.

The first thing Bobby saw as he was pulled through the door was the one-armed man, standing at the foot of a dappled bed. The mattress was spattered and stained with blood. The fan once more thundered to a start. Before Bobby could think his next thought, he felt a hand on his back, forcing him down onto the squalid mattress.

"Turn your face to the wall," the tall man said. "And bite down on the pillow, boy. You'll be glad I told you to."

Bobby was stricken with waves of revulsion as he bit down on the filthy pillow. When he turned his head, he saw that the wall, too, was spattered with dried brown bloodstains. His whole body tensed. Over the din of the fan, he heard what sounded like a rubber sole pivoting on the cement floor. And then the sickening whooshing sound of a whip.

The first blows were so fierce that Bobby was momentarily stunned. After four or five cracks, his back felt as if it were on fire. He turned his face to see a thick leather strap, with grooved metal in the center, slicing through the air toward him. He braced himself. Whoosh. Crack. His skin was ripping. Whoosh. He tried to get up, but the tall man slammed him back down onto the bed. Each blow forced his small body deeper into the bed. Fifteen lashes. Twenty.

"God help me," Bobby cried.

"You'll shut up if you know what's good for you, boy."

Bobby felt a warm liquid running down his legs. Was it pee or blood? He counted, he thought, thirty lashes. Each lash tore his flesh until, finally, thankfully, everything went black.

Later, Bobby wasn't sure how long it had been, he awakened under a spray of cold water. He knew instantly that he was back at his cottage, in the locker room showers. He was naked, except for the scraps of underwear enmeshed in the bloody flesh of his backside.

His nightmare had just begun.

For two days, Robert lived alone in his consciousness, remembering things he spent his whole life forgetting. He did not leave the house, or answer the telephone. The memories came easier than he had anticipated, easier than he would have liked, and now all he could think about was that year at the Florida School for Boys.

It was all so dreadfully clear. The savage beatings. The rapes. The terror in boys' eyes when they were awakened in the middle of the night and hauled off to the dingy building they called the White House. The boys always came back looking as if they had seen a ghost. Some didn't come back at all.

Robert remembered hearing stories on campus. Stories about runaways being caught and beaten to death. Stories about the boys who lived on the African-American side being treated even worse than the white boys. "How many boys died while I was there?" he wondered. "And how many died because no one spoke up?"

He needed to tell someone now, to unburden himself from the weight of the gruesome memories and to help assuage the guilt he felt for keeping such a terrible secret.

"Monica," Robert thought, picking up the telephone. "Monica will understand."

Monica Bordes was a teacher in her mid-twenties who worked for Robert when she was a teenager, helping him manage his sales crews. She was less than half Robert's age, but twice her own age in maturity, and a little rough around the edges. The pair bonded over long talks during tedious drives between gigs and had eventually become confidants. The friendship had lasted. Robert felt as if he could talk to Monica about almost anything.

The telephone call began with the usual chatter, his business, her plans to attend law school, each other's vacation plans. Robert was usually happy to listen to Monica babble about this and that, but now he was distracted by the small talk.

"Have you heard about that poor boy that was killed at the Florida boot camp?" he blurted out, cutting off Monica in mid-sentence.

Monica said she had read about Martin Anderson. Of course, she said, everyone had. How could such a tragedy happen? A young boy, dead only two hours after arriving at a youth detention camp. Something just isn't right, she said.

"You know, I was at a place like that," Robert said, haltingly at first. "A place where they beat you with a whip and where I fear they probably killed boys."

"You're kidding, right?" Monica asked, incredulous.

"No," Robert said. "I wish I was."

For the next hour, Robert told Monica things he remembered about the reform school in Marianna. He told her about the ungodly beating he got on his first night there, and about all the missing boys. He described Hatton and Tidwell, and how they used to awaken sleeping boys, accuse them of some made-up offense, then take them to this terrible building they called the White House for their punishment. He wondered whether boys died from those beatings.

"Holy shit, Bob," Monica said. "Why didn't you tell?"

"I was young and I was terrified I'd be sent back there, so I kept my mouth shut," Robert said. "And when I got older, I refused to think about it."

"You ought to do something," she said.

"It's been forty-three years," said Robert. "Who's going to listen now?"

"Somebody needs to know," she said.

CHAPTER THREE

April 2008. The shade trees lining the streets of Greenville's historic district sway gently, back and forth, as if to the rhythm of a sad song. Michael O'McCarthy throws open the living room windows of his storied bungalow on Robinson Street in the South Carolina city. The curtains flutter inward and the spring breeze washes over him, like water from a warm bath.

Bushed from working long hours on his latest project, a documentary about Harriet Tubman, the African-American abolitionist, all he wanted was to brew a pot of his favorite Costa Rican coffee and collapse on the couch. But he had more work to do before indulging in his nighttime ritual.

Michael was a self-made intellectual, a strapping man with rugged good looks who felt every day of his sixty-five hard-fought years. He was already forty-three when he replaced his addiction to Jack Daniel's with a near frantic compulsion to right one or another of society's transgressions.

Until then, he had always seemed on the verge of ruining his life.

In 1963, Michael, just turned twenty, went on a bender and ended up robbing a service station in California for $6.37 worth of gasoline. The police caught up with him before he could reach the Mexican border and he was charged with second-degree robbery.

Unluckily for him, he went before a hanging judge who sentenced him to a year to life in the California Men's Colony, a medium-security prison about halfway between Los Angeles and San Francisco.

Michael used the first three years of his incarceration to educate himself in the subjects of psychology, sociology, and political science.

He was hypnotized by the writings of Karl Marx, Friedrich Engels, and Leon Trotsky, and it was there, in his dingy cell at the CMC, that he chose to adopt the Marxist philosophy of class struggle in order to help achieve a classless society.

His first goal as a revolutionary socialist was to challenge the California prison system, which he saw as corrupt, oppressive, and rife with government-sanctioned racism. The guards at the CMC were predominantly white and they reveled in using race to pit the prisoners against each other. The way Michael saw it, the enemy wasn't black or white. The enemy was the state.

At the same time that Michael found his calling, the burgeoning civil rights movement spawned the more confrontational Black Power movement. The Black Panther Party, whose doctrine was to fight police brutality and racism with acts of social agitation, had found a home in the nation's penal system, fueling the already antagonistic relationship between black prisoners and "the establishment." Michael, a white man in an institution dominated by black prisoners, began to vocalize his support for the Black Panthers and their militant principles.

By 1968, when Huey Newton, the infamous Panther Party's founder, arrived at the CMC, charged with killing an Oakland police officer, Michael had already won the trust of many of the black inmates there. In a secret meeting, he warned Newton of an alleged government plot to target and kill him. Word of the encounter got back to prison officials, who labeled Michael a troublemaker and sent him into solitary confinement. The warden vowed that the only way he would ever leave prison was in a pine box, because the state would never tolerate a "white Eldridge Cleaver" walking its streets.

Later that year, Michael was transferred to the maximum-security Soledad State Prison, where his reputation as a Black Panther sympathizer preceded him. George Jackson, the charismatic founder of the Black Guerrilla Family, a Marxist prison gang, and the prison organizer for the Panthers, welcomed the angry white insurgent into his circle. Michael had come highly recommended by Newton and that was good enough for Jackson. The two men bonded over their shared belief in Marxism and their disdain for the totalitarian prison system. By the time Michael was paroled in December 1969, after serving six years for stealing a tank of gasoline, he and Jackson were close comrades.

Michael was working in a plastics factory and writing anti-government commentary for the alternative *Los Angeles Free Press* in his spare time when, less than a month after his release from prison, on January 16, 1970, he heard on the television news that Jackson and two other black prisoners had been charged with murdering a guard in their maximum-security cellblock. The story circulated by officials was that the killing was in retaliation for the shooting deaths, three days earlier, of three black inmates by a guard during a dispute in the exercise yard.

Teaming up with Jackson's mother, Georgia, and younger brother, Jonathan, Michael helped organize the Soledad Brothers Defense Committee, whose manifesto was to publicize Jackson's case and promote prison reform. But on August 21, 1971, three days before Jackson was to go on trial, he was killed during what officials described as a prison uprising. Some, Michael included, believed his death was a political assassination by the San Quentin prison administration.

Jackson's death marked the beginning of the end of the prisoner movement in California, and it had a profound effect on Michael. Believing that the system was behind the death of his friend, he became paranoid that he, too, was being targeted for political assassination. The authorities were winning the war and the subjugated had lost one of their top commanders.

Disillusioned and defeated, Michael drank more. He couldn't keep a job, or sustain a relationship. One marriage ended, then a second, and a third. His thirties dissolved into a boozy blur of blackouts and missed moments and his forties were headed in that same direction. But then, in 1986, on Sunset Boulevard in West Los Angeles, he was caught driving drunk. He woke up in the drunk tank, humiliated and afraid, and finally saw the light. He still wasn't sure why. That was twenty-two years ago and he hadn't had a drink since.

Now Michael worked the way he once guzzled whiskey, compulsively, obsessively, losing himself in one cause while craving the next.

This messianic need to save the world paid off with recognition more than money.

Six years after he took his last drink, Michael made a name for himself for his role in winning reparations for the nine living African-American survivors of the 1923 Rosewood Massacre.

Rosewood had been a random calling, like all of them. It was sometime in the early nineties that Michael read about the small Florida town where mobs of whites stormed black neighborhoods, burning down homes and killing innocent men, women, and children. Right then he decided that the state of Florida needed to atone for the sins of Rosewood, and he, a thinker with a knack for getting people to listen, could make it happen. Perhaps even to his own surprise, he succeeded.

It was through Michael's efforts to find the victims who were still living, seventy years later, and the publicity generated by their stories, that led to a formal apology by the Florida governor and compensation for the people who suffered. One of the happiest days of Michael's life was in 1994 when Florida governor Lawton Chiles signed the Rosewood Compensation Bill, a $2.1 million package for the survivors and their descendants for what Chiles termed a "blind act of bigotry."

Michael never knew what his next mission would be, but after his Rosewood success, it often began with an e-mail from someone who had heard about his victory.

It was an April 2008 night in South Carolina now, and there was a day's worth of e-mails to be read.

Michael puts aside his thoughts about the Costa Rican coffee and the welcoming couch. Sighing, he drops into his office chair and logs onto his computer. The blowing curtains nip at his neck as he quickly scans the subject line of each new e-mail.

One stops him cold.

"The Florida School for Boys," it says.

His hand quivers, like the leaves on the white oak trees outside his window, and he is hardly able to guide the mouse.

When he finally manages to open the message, he sees it is from a stranger, a Robert Straley, of Clearwater, Florida.

"Dear Sir," it began. "Help us expose the horrors of a place called 'The White House,' where hundreds of boys were raped, flogged and perhaps even murdered. Help us put an end to Florida's most shameful secret." At the end is a postscript: "Sir," it asks, "can you do for us what you did for Rosewood?"

Michael feels as if the oxygen has been sucked out of his lungs. *The White House,* he whispers desperately. The White House. Who is this man? And how does he know?

Bile burns in his throat. As Michael gasped for breath, the words on the computer screen blur into one another, and then he hears the wails of a child. The cries are his own.

CHAPTER FOUR

Jennifer Ziemann threaded through the narrow streets of Greenville's west end, her lean calves pinging, her cheeks ruddy from the nip of the wind.

Running, like art, is her passion. Sometimes, the more difficult it seems, the better she feels. She used to run to get away from her brutal first husband, to escape her claustrophobic life.

Now running is an extension of the way she feels about herself. Strong. Resilient. Loved.

As she turned onto Croft Street, she considered putting in an extra mile, but the hour is late, and Michael was almost certainly home already, waiting with a steaming cup of espresso, ready to share stories from the day.

With seven miles behind her, the willowy brunette stepped up her pace. She passed Croft Park, budding green with spring, then turned left on Robinson Street, and sprinted toward the home she has shared with her husband-to-be for the past year.

As she approached their cottage, she could see that the living room windows were open, the curtains flapping inward. She envisioned Michael waiting inside, a broad smile covering his face, the cup of espresso in his hand, made just the way she likes it, with a teaspoon of sugar.

Michael and Jennifer met, by chance, three years earlier, in May 2005, at their respective sons' ninth-grade orientation at Eastside High School in Greenville. Michael was thrice divorced and living alone in a spacious apartment in town to be near his fourteen-year-son, Michael. Jennifer felt trapped in her second bad marriage.

When their sons introduced them that day at school, it was that old clichéd "sparks flew" kind of scenario. Michael said later that when he first spotted Jennifer, standing in the doorway of the school, in her polka-dot skirt and flip-flops, he literally saw a glow around her. She thought he was one of the most charismatic men she had ever met. The chemistry between them was so potent that neither one paid attention to the thirty-year age difference.

They became acquaintances after that, sharing long conversations about books and art and politics and the like. Michael was drawn to Jennifer's youthful energy and optimism. She saw him as a savior of sorts from her stifling life, a Hemingwayesque mentor who encouraged her to learn and grow.

Their friendship developed during Jennifer's regular visits to Michael's apartment, under the auspices of borrowing books from his vast collection. She couldn't wait to finish each one, so she would have an excuse to return to his place to choose another. Then they would pass the afternoon together, drinking coffee and discussing whichever book one or the other had last read.

Michael showed Jennifer his paintings, island scenes in vivid colors, and allowed her to read his poetry and political essays. He shared stories about the time he spent in prison, before she was born, and about his long commitment to sobriety, and his gradual transformation into the successful social activist he had become.

The accomplished, older man captivated Jennifer. She loved hearing his stories, and he seemed interested in hers. She told him about the small southern town, twenty-five minutes north-west of Atlanta, a place that had a courthouse with a clock tower but little more, where she grew up with parents who couldn't seem to find much to like about her.

She explained that she used to write, and thought she was pretty good, and that she had tried her hand at painting, but only for her own eyes.

After a time, she took a chance and trusted Michael with stories about her violent first marriage, at the age of seventeen, and the terrible beatings she suffered at the hands of her abusive ex-husband. Barely a day had gone by during the seven years they were together, she said, that she hadn't been bloodied or raped or tormented in some way, and she had the scars to prove it.

At first, Jennifer worried that Michael would judge her, but his caring expression told her it was all right to tell. So she told him everything.

Once, she said, after she made her ex-husband his breakfast— "two eggs over easy, don't break the yolks, cream of wheat, not instant, no lumps"—he had struck her unconscious with a serrated crystal bowl. A rainbow of blue, red, and green M&Ms rained on her face, just before the bowl struck her head. As she came to, she heard him say, in an eerily calm voice, "Looks like I might have done it this time, Jennifer."

The last time her former husband broke her nose, he had re-peatedly kicked her in the ribs with his steel-toed work boots as she tried to crawl away. That was when she finally realized she would die if she stayed.

So Jennifer called 911 and her husband was arrested. She had shaken like a willow tree when she was called to testify at his trial, but the jury believed her and he was found guilty of aggra-vated assault and sentenced to six years in state prison. Jennifer went home, packed up her boys, and fled from Georgia to Green-ville to start a new life.

Not long after settling down in her new city, she had met her second husband and, as it turned out, that marriage wasn't much better.

You deserve a better life, Michael had said, encouraging her to pursue her love of painting, and of writing. One day, he promised, she would learn to like herself enough to find happi-ness. That was the only thing Michael had said that she didn't quite believe.

Jennifer found herself feeling closer to Michael than anyone else in her life. They began spending more and more time to-gether. She had never known anyone so "normal," and she had never felt so normal as the times they were together. Michael and Jennifer had found in each other an empathetic friend. Their shared pain bound them even tighter.

Then, out of the blue, Michael told Jennifer, albeit gently, that he needed to step away from the friendship, at least for a while, because he was falling in love with her.

They would have to stop communicating, he said, at least while she was still married, and even if she did ever end up leaving her husband, she needed to take time to heal herself and not jump into another relationship, the way she had done before.

Jennifer was heartbroken. By then, she had felt that Michael was her best friend. With every day that passed with no communication between them, she missed him more. Life without Michael in it was even more unbearable than it had been before she met him.

Lonely and frustrated, she began looking at her second husband with the revulsion of a captive toward a captor. He was the only thing standing between her and the life she craved, the life and the freedom that Michael had shown her she could have.

Her disdain for him bubbled over one night when he was stumbling drunk and began calling her names. That time, rather than retreating to her room and waiting for him to sleep it off, she had gathered up all of her strength, pushed him out of the house, and locked the door behind him.

Later that night, she wrote Michael an e-mail that began:

"I did it. I stood up for myself. He is gone. I am free. I believe congratulations are in order. Ha-Ha. You put no pressure on me and you haven't from the get-go, thank you. Thank you for being my friend, for listening to me, for just sharing a part of you with me, and for making me feel normal. Hell, I almost feel pretty and that is quite an accomplishment."

Jennifer moved into an apartment in Greenville with her two sons, and Michael went against his own advice and resumed their friendship, which evolved into a romantic relationship. They had been together ever since.

Indeed, Jennifer was blindsided one day, not long after they started living together, when she had been doing dishes, nattering on about this and that, and turned to find Michael on bended knee. "Will you marry me?" he had said, laughing and crying as he wrapped her up in his arms.

She had backed away from him that night, uncertain what to make of his proposal. When they decided to live together, a year after she separated from her second husband, they had agreed they were against marriage. Their relationship worked so well because they wanted to be together, not because they were legally bound to each other.

Yes, Michael had said, that was true. But he wanted to make the gesture to show her just how much he loved her.

Jennifer spent weeks afterward wondering what to do with the marriage proposal. She had discussed the pros and cons with her therapist, and turned herself inside out until, one day, she realized she wanted to marry him, too.

The three years she had known Michael had been the best of her life. With Michael's encouragement, she had entered therapy and had taken up painting again. And her talent for writing got her a column in the local alternative weekly newspaper. Her boys, who had seen her pummeled by their father and hadn't seen him since they fled Georgia, embraced Michael, and he was a strong, kindly male figure to them.

Jennifer decided she felt safe and secure enough to be married to a man who stood by her, yet gave her the space to get to know herself. She and Michael fit together, like pieces of a puzzle.

Now, with a month to go before the wedding ceremony, her biggest fear was that the dream would somehow end.

Jennifer bounded up the front steps to the cottage, calling her soon-to-be husband's name.

"Michael? Michael, are you there?"

She kicked off her running shoes and burst through the screen door, expecting to see him standing on the other side.

The house was still.

Michael's office door was ajar, and she glanced inside. He was seated at his computer, with his back to her. She stood in the doorway, and he must have known she was there, but he didn't turn around.

"Michael?" she said. "Michael? Are you okay?"

As she walked toward him, Jennifer saw that Michael had tears streaming down his cheeks. She embraced him. The only time she had ever seen Michael cry was when he proposed to her, and then he was laughing and crying. And then they were both laughing and crying.

These were bitter tears.

"I can't believe this," Michael said, his voice, strangely fearful, as he stared at the message on the computer screen. "I can't believe this. I can't believe this."

"What is it, Michael?" Jennifer asked, alarmed. "What's happened?"

Michael, her rock, the gentle man who preached openness and sharing and truthfulness, didn't acknowledge her. He stared straight ahead, his face compressed into an angry grimace, his fingernails digging into the palms of his hands, shutting her out.

Jennifer had never seen this Michael. And standing there she knew that, while she was out, her idyllic life had suddenly changed.

———

Michael didn't eat or sleep much for the next few days. Most of the time, he stayed shut in his office for hours at a time. When he did emerge, he was sullen and detached.

He seemed to have aged ten years since the night Jennifer found him, crying, at his computer.

He had finally shown her the e-mail from Straley, asking him for help in exposing the Florida School for Boys. Jennifer knew something about Michael's experience at the same reform school. He had written about it, twenty-eight years earlier, for an upstart political magazine called *Southern Exposure*. It was one of the essays he had invited her to read during the early days of their friendship.

In 1980, when Michael wrote the piece, he thought he needed to purge his haunting memories of Marianna before he could even attempt getting sober. He had written the account in the third person, as if he were telling someone else's story. And what he had written was a mere hint at what he experienced there.

After the publication of that article, Michael had never spoken of Marianna again, not even with Jennifer when she asked him about it after reading the story. There were things he had been through, and things he had seen there, that had been too terrible to write about, and too awful to resurrect without the potential for losing himself in alcohol, or cocaine, or pills.

So, for the sake of his sobriety, for the sake of his sanity, Michael had erased his memories of Marianna. Memories of other boys, snatched from their bunks in the middle of the night and dragged off to a squat, dank building called the White House, where unspeakable acts of cruelty had taken place. Memories of being lined up, sometimes with one or two other boys, and forced to listen to the screams of whomever was the first to be beaten and tortured by the malicious men who were paid by the state to be their keepers. Knowing that when the screams stopped, it could be his turn.

Michael was fifteen when he was sentenced to spend a year in Marianna. What haunted him the most, and the memory he had buried so deep he believed it could never be resurrected, involved the night he and a friend he knew only as Woody were delivered to the White House to be punished for running away.

It was 1958, summertime, if his senses served him, because he still remembered the smell of rotting manure that fertilized the surrounding farmers' fields, as he was dragged to the tiny building by school director Robert Hatton.

Michael was taken into the punishment room first, while Woody waited. Hatton did the beating and it was agonizing. A houseman named Dixon was instructed to hold Michael down. Michael heard Hatton's boots pivot on the concrete floor, and the whip hit the ceiling, then the wall, before it bit into his back and his buttocks, spraying his blood on the walls. Every blow drove him deeper into the metal springs of the bloody mattress, and deeper into a gray hole of semiconsciousness.

He didn't know how much later it was when he awakened to Hatton's cold voice. "Get up, boy," the director said. "I said, get on up."

Michael tried to shift his legs, to pull himself up off the bed, but he couldn't move. "If you don't get up like I told you, we're going to start all over again," Hatton said. "Now." Pulling against the bed frame, Michael eventually raised himself to a crouching position. Dixon accompanied him as he limped into the dank hallway and, as instructed, stood facing the wall.

It was Woody's turn.

Michael braced himself. The grind of the industrial fan did little to muffle the tortured cries of his beleaguered friend. "No more!" Woody wailed. "Please! Oh please, God, no more!" Michael sank to his knees. He swore he heard Woody's blood splattering on the walls.

Twenty strikes. Thirty. He could hear the sounds of a scuffle breaking out. "Get him back on his stomach," Michael heard the assistant superintendent shout. Forty strikes. Woody's screams had become one long unbroken wail. Fifty strikes. Fifty-five. The more Woody screamed, the more he was beaten.

Michael covered his ears and screamed for Woody, screamed until he could no longer hear his friend, begging for mercy.

And when he could no longer scream, Michael sang. He sang a song he had learned as a very young child. He sang softly, so only he could hear. "This little light of mine, I'm gonna let it shine . . . Everywhere I go . . . Shine, shine, shine."

He sang to keep his own sanity.

What Michael had never written, had never told anyone, was that he never saw Woody after that night. And for the past fifty years he had blamed himself. Blamed himself for not standing up to the evil men who branded children with their brutality, the way plantation owners had bullied and beaten their slaves into submission.

Had what happened to boys in Marianna been different from, for instance, the beating described by W. L. Bost, a slave from North Carolina, for the Federal Writers' Project in 1937?

"I remember how they kill one nigger whippin' him with the bull whip. Many the poor nigger nearly killed with the bull whip.

But this one die. He was a stubborn Negro and didn't do as much work as his Massa though he ought to. He been lashed lot before. So they take him to the whippin' post, and then they strip his clothes off and then the man stan' off and cut him with the whip. His back was cut all to pieces. The cuts about half inch apart. Then after they whip him they tie him down and put salt on him. Then after he lie in the sun awhile they whip him agin. But when they finish with him he was dead."

When Hatton was finished with Woody, was he dead? Why else had he never been seen on campus after that night?

More than anything else, Michael blamed himself for doing nothing to stop the brutal flogging of his friend.

Because he couldn't live with that guilt, he had drunk it down, and then, in order to save himself, he had censored it from his mind.

Now this man named Straley had forced him to face his memories, and he wasn't sure he would survive it.

Three days after he received the e-mail, Michael picked up the telephone and dialed Straley's number in Clearwater.

One ring. Two. The answering machine clicked on. Relief. "Hello, this is Robert. Please leave a message and I'll call you back when I return."

Michael almost hung up, but he pulled the telephone receiver back to his lips.

There was no turning back to the way things were before Straley entered his life, he knew that. Every night since then, he had awakened, shivering, feeling as if the hands that came so close to defeating him as a child were reaching for him again. And he felt just as helpless as that boy did, facing his adult torturers.

"Yes. Hello. My name is Michael O'McCarthy and I believe you sent me an e-mail," he said, his voice cautious and edgy. "I can hardly believe that I got this. It's the last thing I've ever expected. This is a fifty-year nightmare that I thought I had put behind me and here it is. This was the last thing I expected to be dumped in my lap. You can't imagine the nightmare this has brought back to me.

"I'm not sure I can help you, but I'll leave my number in case you want to call me back."

Michael took a long breath.

"I hope he never calls," he said to himself as he hung up the phone. "I want this to go away."

CHAPTER FIVE

*Y*es. Hello. My name is Michael O'McCarthy and I believe you sent
me an e-mail. . . . I can hardly believe that I got this. . . .

Robert punched the play button on his telephone answering
machine, trying to make sense of what he just heard.

"You can't imagine the nightmare this has brought back to me. . . ."

He took a deep breath, and blew it out. Was he interpreting
the message correctly? he wondered. Could it be?

In the months since Robert had confided in his friend Monica,
he had been consumed by his memories of Marianna.

On that first day they talked, Monica had done a computer
search of the reform school and discovered that a man from
Georgia had a similar story.

"You won't believe it," she had cried, when she called to tell
Robert what she found.

"Robert! You have to see this! You have to get hold of this
guy. His story is just like yours."

At first, Robert had mixed emotions about Monica's discovery.

In one way, he felt vindicated by what she found. He wasn't the only one making the kind of claims so sordid that they seemed almost inconceivable.

But more than forty years had passed, and it was more than likely that the perpetrators of the abuses at Marianna were dead. He began to have second thoughts about his initiative. What was the use of digging up the past? What good could come of it? he had asked Monica, somewhat reluctantly. Better to move beyond it, he said.

But the ghosts of Marianna wouldn't let go.

Still haunted by his childhood memories, Robert had finally gathered enough courage to contact the Georgia man.

The man told Robert that he posted his story on the Internet because, after all these years, he had never been able to shake Marianna. The effects of the place were corrosive and incessant.

He was sure there were others out there who could be helped by sharing their memories, the man had said, but he hadn't had much luck getting men to respond.

Robert had been one of the first.

The Georgia man wanted his so-called caretakers at Marianna, the men who committed atrocities in the name of discipline, especially Tidwell and Hatton, to be punished for all the harm he claimed they had done.

He had firsthand knowledge, he said, of boys who had died from beatings in the White House, and he believed the bodies of dozens, maybe hundreds of boys, many who were caught trying to run away from their captors, were buried in the fields and swamplands surrounding the reform school.

Robert was stunned. He knew of boys who ran away, under the cover of darkness, guided only by moonlight and the flow of the Chipola River. It was true that some had never come back, and there were always rumors of boys being killed, but he had never wanted to believe it.

He still didn't.

The whole town knew when a boy escaped. Each time it happened, almost always in the middle of the night, a shrill siren echoed for miles, from the tree-lined streets of the neighborhoods in town to the farms along the meandering Chipola. The sound of the siren was usually followed by the yelps of bloodhounds, tracking along the grassy banks of the river.

Runaways didn't have much chance of making it out of Marianna, but that didn't stop boys from trying.

With fifty-dollar bounties on their heads, if the guards and the dogs couldn't catch them, the local farmers were more than willing to pitch in.

Indeed, boy hunting had become a sport of sorts in Marianna.

The sirens blew, and farmers sprang from their beds and out into the night, the beams of their flashlights cutting through the rows of lima beans and corn sprouting in their fields. If they were lucky, they could catch a boy, collect their money, and still begin doing chores by sunup.

When a boy disappeared from the reform school, a letter, signed by whomever was superintendent at the time, was sent to his parent or legal guardian, stating: "It is with regret that I must inform you that your son ran away from the school and as yet we have not been able to locate him."

Robert wondered how many parents had just accepted the

word of authorities that their sons had run away. How many boys who were named in those brief, typewritten letters had really escaped? Had some been murdered? And if so, how many bodies were buried on the Marianna campus? How many bones were concealed in silt at the bottom of the Chipola River?

"I should have said something years ago," Robert said to himself, suddenly overwhelmed by the idea that, had someone spoken out decades earlier, lives might have been saved.

"My God, this could still be going on."

Were boys still in danger at Marianna now, Robert wondered, and at other institutions around the state and the country? Boys who were too afraid to tell, the way he had been, more than four decades ago, for fear no one would believe their stories, and they would be forced to face their abusers again?

How could he continue to keep the secret of Marianna when there was a chance that boys' lives might still be at stake?

The answer was, he couldn't.

For the next few months, Robert worked from daybreak until bedtime, researching the Florida School for Boys. The information he dug up was stunning. Hardly a year had passed since 1903 when there wasn't a scorching indictment of the institution, either in a newspaper or a government report. Robert had read with disbelief stories with headlines such as "A Monstrosity," and "Fourteen Hundred Acres of Hell," and "Bulldoze Them to the Ground." After a tour of the school in 1968, Florida governor Claude Kirk was quoted in the *St. Petersburg Times* as saying, "If one of your kids were kept in such circumstances, you'd be up there with rifles."

So the secret of Marianna had hardly been a secret, after all. Everyone from governors to legislators to journalists had known the place was a hellhole. Still, the abject cruelty to children had been allowed to continue year after year, decade after decade. Why? Robert wondered. Was it because the public considered them throwaway children and not worth fighting for? Or was it that the children had no voice, so it was easy for people to pretend they didn't exist? It was easy to toss your outrage out with the morning paper, but the sound of a child's voice was much harder to ignore.

More than ever before, Robert was determined to be that voice; for himself, and for all the boys who had been caught in the state's vast web of child exploitation. He just had to find a way to get people to listen.

It wasn't until late March 2008, more than a year after he had read in the morning paper of the young boy's death in a Florida boot camp, when he came across an old story from the *Panama City Pilot* archives, that Robert felt he had enough ammunition to entice the media with his story.

The story, entitled "Florida's Disgrace," ran in the February 2, 1922, edition of the paper. It told of a young man named Martin Talbert, from North Dakota, who had been arrested for hopping a ride on a freight train near Tallahassee. While he was in custody, Talbert had been flogged fifty times with a leather strap. When he was told to get up and couldn't, the whip master gave him fifty lashes more. The beating had left Talbert skinned raw from his neck to his knees, and he died from his injuries. His death stirred a national outrage, and in 1923, the state of Florida outlawed the flogging of prisoners. Yet the Florida School for Boys was flogging children more than forty years later. Robert had experienced it himself in 1963. And the reform school was still operating as a "residential commitment facility," renamed the Arthur G. Dozier School for Boys, after a former superintendent. Who was to say that boys were not still being flogged at Marianna?

Robert felt as if Martin Talbert was speaking to him from the grave. It was time to take his story public so that all the boys at Marianna and places like it would not have suffered and died in vain.

Robert spent the next three days gathering the names of influential people to contact for help. If just one newspaper or television station picked up his story, men might come forward, strengthening the case against the reform school and corporal punishment of children everywhere. There had to be countless others who were carrying around a lifetime of wreckage, Robert figured, all because a few sadistic officials had turned misguided boys into jaded, angry men. He just needed to find them.

The 141 names that Robert compiled were names of journalists, child advocates, and social activists he had culled from the Internet during late-night computer searches. Michael O'McCarthy had been a name that popped up during one of those searches. He was listed as a contributor to the *Los Angeles Free Press,* a small, alternative newspaper that had recently been revived after a thirty-year hiatus. Robert had gone on to read about O'McCarthy's role in Rosewood, which he remembered reading about years earlier. He added O'McCarthy's name to his e-mail list almost as an afterthought, then had added the personal line, asking "Can you do for us what you did for Rosewood?"

Robert poured himself a generous glass of red wine and played the message from O'McCarthy one last time. No matter how many times he played it, he heard the same thing. If O'McCarthy was saying what he thought he was—that he, too, was a victim of Marianna—it was a freak coincidence that had brought them together.

Draining his glass, Robert picked up the telephone and dialed South Carolina.

The voice on the other end of the phone sounded weary.

"Hello. This is Michael O'McCarthy."

"It's Robert Straley. Do you have a minute to talk?"

Michael was reassured by the sound of the soft-spoken Southerner's voice, but he was cautious nevertheless.

"When I sent you that e-mail, I had no idea you had been in Marianna," Robert said.

In the hour that followed, the men forged the kind of sudden connection that can only come from shared pain, each recalling difficult memories from Marianna.

"I'll never forget how scared I was on my first trip to the White House," Michael said. "I thought they were going to kill me."

For his whole adult life, Robert said, he has dared death, he believed, as punishment for not standing up to his persecutors in Marianna. Once, he had taken a fifty-foot dive off a cliff in Jamaica into shallow water, while a group of stunned natives looked on. He raced his motorcycle on the 101 from Santa Barbara to Oxnard, taking curves at breakneck speeds, and frequently swerving into the shoulder, with only a few inches between him and the bike and the steep cliffs jutting down to the ocean below. The closest he had come to losing the dare was in Ochos

Rios, when he ventured out to a coral reef as a swarm of black storm clouds rolled into the harbor. Swimming desperately against the current, in choppy water, he had spent all of his energy, and almost given up hope of getting back, when the wind turned and the tide pushed him to the seawall. None of it helped relieve the feelings of shame and cowardice left over from the Florida School for Boys.

"I wish I could have been braver," Robert told Michael. "But I screamed and cried and begged for mercy. They scared me in a way I had never known. They put shame in my heart and I'm still trying to prove I'm not a coward."

The beatings he endured "were beatings that filled me with a rage that I have lived with ever since. A rage I would, in turn, take out on others, although I could not have imagined it lying on that bloodstained bed in the White House."

The men talked the next day and the next, feeling each other out, each time trusting a little bit more. On the third day, Robert called Michael in tears.

"Did you know about the rape room?" he asked.

"No, I don't," Michael replied.

Robert had been taken there by two guards. He remembered being pushed facedown onto a mattress. One of the men kneed him in the back, while the other brutalized him. He had passed out and awakened back in his bunk.

It was no wonder Robert woke up every morning thinking there was a man sitting on the end of his bed.

"I'm so sorry, Robert," Michael said. "I had no idea."

On that same night, Michael sat down at his computer and typed out an answer to Straley's request.

SUBJECT: The White House

For years after my visit to the White House in 1958, I buried the experience with alcohol, then drugs, while the rage raged. . . . When I look back at the crusades I have forged or participated in—Civil Rights, Prisoner Rights, Veterans Rights, Rosewood—I know now that, other than a sense of humanity, it was the rage against the injustice we suffered at the Florida School for Boys that drove me. I dealt with what happened to me in Marianna with drinking and anger . . . never sorrow. Never sobbing, as I have these last two days. Now it is very difficult for me to write even this without crying, wanting to lapse into sobs.

There will come a time to share the pain—as survivors of this monstrous legacy of official torture and cruel and inhuman punishment. Our story is handicapped by time. It is handicapped by witness: We need as many men, black and white, to make this story public.

I will do the best I can to help you bring this thing to light.

Are you sure you want to do this? Jennifer had asked her anguished husband-to-be.

This is *my* Rosewood, Michael thought as he hit SEND.

CHAPTER SIX

Marianna is a culture apart from the iconic beaches and carnal nightlife that attract people from around the world to the Sunshine State. Situated in the heart of Jackson County, in the Florida Panhandle, the town looks and feels more like rural Alabama, twenty miles north.

A small sign leading to Marianna's downtown calls it "the city of Southern charm." In some ways, it is. Antebellum homes, nestled on small, verdant squares, embrace a bountiful main street where cozy storefronts burst with colored awnings and a Confederate monument stands tall on the Jackson County Courthouse lawn. Canopies of poplar and oak trees shade cloistered neighborhoods, and children still draw hopscotch courts on the sidewalks with pastel-colored chalk. On sultry summer evenings, people rock on their wraparound porches, swatting flies and sipping icy glasses of sweet tea.

In many ways, the essence of Marianna is as it was back in 1938, when the author Frank Shay wrote, "Saturday is Marianna's big day, when the rural folks come to trade and do their week's shopping, and for that day there is a degree of activity that has its attractiveness. The balance of the week it is, at best, a very dull town."

For the most part, the people of Marianna are not highly educated; three in four are high school graduates, but only one in five have college degrees. Nor do most people make a lot of money. The estimated annual income for residents of the city is $20,000 below Florida's average. And for every Greek Revival home downtown, a trailer home resides on the fringes.

Life is simple. Preachers fill Sunday services, and family life often revolves around church-sponsored activities—bingo on Tuesdays, three-dollar pulled chicken barbecue suppers on Wednesdays, and Friday-night Bible class.

With a population of 6,200, Marianna looks like a picture postcard for quintessential Americana, with people who care about God, country, and family.

It is also a city with a shameful past.

Northwest Florida was a no-man's-land in 1818, when General Andrew Jackson and his troops pushed through during the campaign to seize the Spanish colony and, at the same time, drive the Seminole Indians from the region. Three years later, when Spain ceded the colony to the United States, many of Jackson's men returned to the region to put down stakes. The narrow slice of terrain lying just south of the Alabama and Georgia borders was initially divided into two counties, St. Johns and Escambia. A third was formed in 1822 when Jackson carved out a share of the two existing counties and named it for himself.

Land speculators soon began arriving in the northwest

wilderness, including the Scottish-born Robert Beveridge, who traveled from Baltimore in 1827 to purchase chunks of the fledgling third county. Beveridge designed a village on a scenic ridge overlooking the Chipola River and, merging his wife's middle name, Maria, with the first name of his business partner's wife, Anna, called it Marianna.

The early settlers had lofty ambitions for the little city. By promising free land, the building of a courthouse, and a public square, Marianna overtook the nearby squatter's town of Webbville to reign as the county seat.

Over the next few decades, Jackson County flourished as a plantation society. Its economy was fueled by agriculture, which relied heavily on the slave trade. When the Civil War broke out in 1861, Florida had more than sixty-one thousand slaves. "The vast majority of the slave population resided in the counties of middle Florida (most in Gadsden, Leon, Jefferson, and Madison counties) and one West Florida county (Jackson), where their labor accounted for 85 percent of the state's cotton production as well as a wide variety of other agricultural crops," R. Boyd Murphree wrote in "Florida and the Civil War: A Short History."

By then, Marianna had grown into "a politically powerful city" that served as both a supply base and a recruiting center for the Confederacy, according to local historian and author Dale Cox. Confederate governor John Milton was part of the plantation aristocracy, residing on a 2,600-acre estate near town.

The war came to Marianna on September 27, 1864, when 850 Union soldiers, including two Negro regiments, raided the city "at high noon" and found themselves challenged by "a rag tag command of Confederate cavalry, reservists and local volunteers," Cox wrote in his book *The Battle of Marianna*. "When the smoke cleared, some 18 men lay dead or dying, 32 were wounded and dozens were being herded away as prisoners."

In the context of the war between the North and the South, the battle of Marianna would be remembered as a tiny raid, but one that dealt a devastating blow to the social, culture, and economic life of the community. St. Luke's Episcopal Church was burned and the city was plundered. Some of Marianna's most prominent citizens were imprisoned up north in Elmira, where many died.

Seven months after the battle, on April 1, 1865, with the end of the Confederacy imminent, Milton took a gun to his own head at his plantation home. Death was apparently preferable to reunion with the states and a life without slaves. Milton was buried in St. Luke's Cemetery in town. The war was all but over, yet Jackson County's bloodiest battle was still to come.

The period of Reconstruction that followed the war saw a constant battle of wills between bitter Southern whites who struggled to maintain the status quo and the freed slaves who groped for the new rights that had been promised them. Jackson County was a powder keg in the aftermath of the war. The county had suffered staggering economic and social losses. The privilege and prestige of the plantation society had been terminally undermined, and the Southern aristocracy diminished. In his book *Anatomy of a Lynching,* James McGovern wrote, "The Reconstruction period in Jackson County produced unusually angry feelings toward blacks and federal officials who legislated radical changes on their behalf. Citizens determined to maintain white supremacy initiated a reign of terror which took more than 150 lives vigilante style in two years."

The opening salvo of what would become known as the Jackson County War was fired on February 27, 1869, in Marianna, according to Daniel R. Weinfeld, an authority on the conflict. Late that evening, Dr. John Finlayson and his friend William Purman, both Reconstruction sympathizers, were shot as they crossed the town square after attending a minstrel performance. Finlayson was struck in the head and died almost instantly. Purman barely survived the shot that passed through his neck and jaw. Although people in town knew the names of the assassins, no one was ever held accountable for the attack.

The shooting would trigger what was to become one of the bloodiest uprisings in the Reconstruction-era South, as gangs of whites and blacks went to war with each other. In his account of the local strife, Cox wrote: "Murders, political assassinations, assaults and bitter reprisals were the tactics of the day and over a period of several years, the Northwest Florida county literally became the scene of a bloodbath as bad as any in Missouri and Kansas during the years before the war."

When the Long Depression of 1873 set in, Northerners began to lose interest in Southern reform and the era of Reconstruction soon faded. By the 1880s, the white elite was restored to power, and African Americans lost most of their civil rights.

Fifty years later, Marianna would put itself at the center of another nefarious chapter of American history with the public lynching of Claude Neal.

A twenty-three-year-old black farmhand who grew up in Jackson County, Neal was tortured, mutilated, and hanged from an oak tree on the courthouse lawn in 1934 in this City of Southern Charm.

Neal had been accused of raping and murdering a young white

woman, Lola Cannidy, when she tried to break off their affair. He was kidnapped from authorities by a swarm of angry men, castrated, burned with hot irons, and stabbed, over and over, even after he was dead. Witnesses to the horror claimed that even small children participated, poking him with whittled sticks.

After hours of torture, Neal's savaged body was tied to the back of a car and dragged to the courthouse, where a large crowd of men, women, and children waited to observe the official lynching.

The event had been advanced in newspapers across the South, attracting people from near and far to the Panhandle city.

"Big Preparation Made for Lynching Tonight," the *Macon Telegraph* wrote in its morning edition on October 26, 1934.

> This morning a mob seized Claude Neal, 23, from a jail in Brewton, Ala., where he had been held in connection with the murder of white girl which took place here several days ago.
>
> At noon a "Committee of Six" representing the mob announced a timetable for the lynching, which was given in newspapers and over the radio as follows:
>
> At sundown the Negro will be taken to the farm two miles from here where Miss Lola Cannidy, the murder victim, lived. There, he will be mutilated by the girl's father.
>
> Then he will be brought to a pigpen in the middle of a cotton field nearby, where the girl's body was found, and killed.
>
> Finally his body will be brought to Marianna, the county seat, nine miles from here, and hung in the court house square for all to see.
>
> "All white folks are invited to the party," said the announcement issued by the mob's Committee of Six.

The next day's papers reported the event in all of its gruesome detail.

"Lynching Carried Off Almost As Advertised," read the headline in the *Birmingham Post* in Alabama.

> Marianna, Fla.—The body of Claude Neal, 23, negro, confessed attacker and slayer of a white girl, swung from a tree on the courthouse lawn here today, victim of an enraged mob's vengeance.... Photographers say they will soon have pictures of the body for sale for fifty cents each. Fingers and toes from Neal's body are freely exhibited on street corners here.

Walter White, the spokesman for the National Association for the Advancement of Colored People (NAACP), would call the lynching "one of the most bestial crimes ever committed by a mob."

But for some, the ghastly pubic execution hadn't been sufficient to avenge Lola Cannidy's death.

When the county sheriff cut down Neal's body, people gathered together to protest and demanded the corpse be strung up again.

The sheriff refused, and for the next two days mobs swarmed downtown Marianna, hunting the frightened blacks that remained there, driving them from their homes and their businesses.

By the time the National Guard was called in to restore order to the Jackson County seat, some two hundred African Americans, mothers and fathers, children and grandparents, had been injured in violent attacks.

In the book *Anatomy of a Lynching*, author James R. McGovern quotes a reporter from a Montgomery, Alabama, newspaper describing the aftermath: "Marianna goes on her placid way apparently unaware of the drama that has attracted the attention of a nation," he said. That same peculiar sentiment was captured in McKay Jenkins's *The South in Black and White: Race, Sex and Literature in the 1940s*. "Despite the horrific and extremely public nature of the lynching, the town of Marianna returned to a kind of stunned calm," Jenkins wrote.

Then there was the chilling firsthand account of Howard Kester, a white minister who visited Marianna to investigate the lynching at the behest of the NAACP. "On the whole," Kester wrote in his 1934 summary, "the lynching was accepted . . . as a righteous act."

As with the shooting of Finlayson and Purman, the town once again circled its wagons and Neal's murder went unpunished.

It was this Marianna that allowed institutional cruelty and perhaps even murder at the Florida School for Boys to continue for decades.

CHAPTER SEVEN

People say something happens when you cross the Apalachicola River, heading west across Florida's Panhandle. You lose an hour on your watch but decades in time.

Jack Levine felt it on a splendid late spring afternoon in 1979 when he motored from his new home in Tallahassee to the Florida School for Boys that first time.

Levine was a young schoolteacher from the Bronx who had followed love to Tallahassee the previous summer. A friend had told him about a teaching job at a state-run adolescent rehabilitation center in the city, and he had started work there that fall.

For months, he had wanted to make the trip west to the Marianna reform school, ever since that first student had told him, "Oh that Marianna, it's a bad place." If he'd heard it once, he'd heard it a dozen times in the few months he had been teaching in Florida. What had really troubled him was that even a mention of being sent there could induce full-fledged panic in his students.

So on that Sunday in May, the twenty-seven-year-old educator had borrowed a friend's car and drove the seventy miles from Tallahassee to the provincial town of Marianna.

Nothing prepared him for what he found there.

Levine pulled up to reform school at around three-thirty that afternoon. His credentials from the state's health and rehabilitative services department got him a wave through the main gate. He parked his borrowed car in the first lot he saw. Before he could push the car door open, a man wearing khaki pants, a blue button-down shirt, and a fixed scowl approached.

"Who are you and what do you want?" the burly man asked.

Levine flashed his ID badge and attempted to smile.

"I'm with HRS. I've never been here and I just wanted to look around."

That's it, he thought, subconsciously reaching for the car keys in his pocket. No way I'm getting any further than this.

To Levine's astonishment, the man just shrugged, as if to say "Have at it," then he walked off.

Levine started walking around campus. He had heard from his students about a supposed isolation building they called the lockup. His kids had said they had friends who were imprisoned there. Bad things happened, they said. Things so bad you don't want to know.

Levine saw it almost immediately, about a hundred yards behind the main administration building—a squat, ramshackle rectangle, windowless, with a heavy metal door.

The lockup, he thought.

He knocked.

The metal door swung out to reveal a colossal man. Levine guessed him at around 240 pounds. The buttons on his blue shirt strained against his massive paunch, and his teeth were rotten.

His manner was flat, detached, slow, and Levine could tell he was put out, annoyed even, by having an unexpected guest.

What do you *wont?* he asked, his northwest Florida drawl a giveaway that he was a local.

Levine held up his ID badge. He wanted to get inside the building in the worst way, but he feared he wouldn't get past the big, cranky guard. He smiled a nonthreatening smile, one he hoped conveyed something like, *Oh I'm new, just here to look around. I don't want to be here anymore than you do. It's just part of the job.*

The guard stepped aside and Levine entered. The first thing that hit him was the shocking combination of murkiness and stench. The place was barely lit. Levine squinted in an effort to see anything. The smell was a pungent blend of body odor and urine. He tried to hold his breath.

The guard took his place at a high table just inside the entrance. His post, Levine thought. The only thing on the table was a leather-bound copy of the Holy Bible. Beyond the guard, Levine saw a narrow hall with two dozen cells, twelve to the left, twelve to the right. The cell doors each had slip bolts, top and bottom. The only opening into each cell was a narrow slot, probably for passing in food, Levine thought.

Levine stood there, stunned. The place reminded him of pictures of concentration camps he had seen. The faint sound of small voices distracted him from his revulsion.

"Who's in here?" he asked.

"Kids," the guard said, never looking up.

"I want to meet one," Levine said, trying his best to sound indifferent.

The guard didn't object, and Levine randomly chose a cell about a third of the way down, on the left side of the hall.

"How about this one?" he asked.

The guard slid the bottom lock open. Clank. He pushed the top lock. It was stuck. Using the force of his two hundred plus pounds, the guard pushed at the lock until he groaned from the effort, but he still couldn't budge it.

A thought flashed in Levine's head: *When was the last time the damn thing was opened?*

"Wait a minute," the guard said, turning to walk back to his post.

The guard returned with the Bible and whacked at the lock, once, twice, three times, until it finally jerked open.

Levine pulled open the door. Something moved, he couldn't tell what it was. He blinked hard, trying to adjust his eyes to be able to see inside the cell. A moment passed, and finally he made it out, a form crouched in the far right corner.

It was a boy, a very small, very frightened boy, perhaps ten or eleven years old. He was wearing only pajama bottoms, no top, and he was coiled up on a bare concrete slab. He was shivering, Levine wasn't sure if it was from fear or the chill of the cold concrete. His head had been shaved bald.

Levine stepped toward the boy.

"Hello," he said. "I'm just here visiting."

The boy cowered.

"I can't help you, but I won't hurt you," Levine said, trying to comfort the boy, but not wanting to give him false hope.

The boy said nothing.

"How long has he been here?" Levine asked.

"For a while," the guard said.

"Why is his head shaved?" Levine asked.

"Because he was pulling his hair out," the guard replied.

———

The Florida School for Boys was built between 1898 and 1900 on twelve hundred acres at an expense of $1,400 in cash, bid by community leaders whose reasons were more practical than altruistic.

The reform school meant work for people in the remote province of northwest Florida, a setting the late author Frank Shay once described as "a down at the heels sort of place," where "wages are low and morals do not achieve an altogether high."

The first scandal at the reform school broke in 1903, three years after taking in its first students.

During those early years, the school housed boys as young as five years old. Their offenses were minor, things like truancy and incorrigibility. In some cases, they were simply unwanted. The legislature had envisioned the reform school as "not simply a place of correction," but a regimented educational program that separated troubled boys from hardened criminals in adult prisons, and taught them to become good citizens.

But members of a joint committee charged with inspecting the fledging institution delivered disturbing news to the Florida senate in the fall of 1903. The school was a failure, the committee reported during an evening session of the legislature in Tallahassee. What the inspectors found in Marianna was nothing like the model that had been envisioned in 1897, when law mandated the idea for the state's first reform school. Rather, the panel reported, "We found [the inmates] in irons, just as common criminals, which in the judgment of our committee, is not the meaning of a 'State Reform School.'"

Marianna, they said, "Is nothing more or less than a prison . . . we recommend that the inmates of said school be more humanely treated, and that the superintendent be required to remove the shackles from the inmates . . . and some other less cruel method be provided for keeping them within the confines of the institution."

If efforts were made to treat the boys with more benevolence after that initial inspection by state investigators, it didn't last long. Members of another investigative committee visited the school in 1911 and reported back to the state capitol in Tallahassee that "the inmates were at times unnecessarily and brutally punished, the instrument of punishment being a leather strap fastened to a wooden handle" (the same type of weapon used for punishment during the 1950s and 1960s, when Robert Straley and Michael O'McCarthy were flogged there).

Three years after the 1911 report, on November 18, 1914, eight boys burned to death in a dormitory fire on the Marianna campus while their keepers were in town "on a pleasure bent," according to official reports. The boys were trapped behind fire escape doors that had been locked to ensure that no one slipped away during the night.

The Jackson County grand jury that investigated the school, after the fire, found that the deaths were due to the "gross carelessness, negligence and mismanagement" by Superintendent W. H. Bell and members of his staff.

An editorial in the *Miami Herald* captured the breadth of the tragedy.

> Clifford Jenkins, 15 years old, was the son of a widow from Clearwater, and no other charge other than playing truant from school was lodged against him when he was sent to the reform school. . . . For playing truant from school a

boy is placed within the care of the state, under the law. The state places him in a building where there is insufficient fire protection. . . . It sends the boys to the third story of the building and, to make matters certain for the inevitable horror, locks them in so they have to climb through a skylight to obtain safety.

Some of them had not the time to save their lives.

It is said that the state can do no wrong. The people of Florida would be glad to know that the state is not responsible for the death of those eight boys who lost their lives in the Marianna fire. Furthermore, they want to be assured that the investigation into the accident is thorough and the responsibility for the accident will be fixed.

The grand jury believed there was plenty of blame to go around. The reform school, it said in its January 5, 1915, report, may have been conceived with good intentions, but the lack of oversight and the indifference to the children by everyone from the Florida legislature to the school employees were to blame for its reprehensible state.

"We find that the legislature has been scanty in its provision for the welfare and maintenance of these children," the grand jury wrote. "We find that they have not been provided with adequate clothing to make them comfortable, we find that punishment which has been allowed to be inflicted, and which has been inflicted, has gone to the extent of being cruel and inhuman, we find that the board of managers have accepted such position under the law requiring them to meet at the school at stated periods, we believe that this board of managers is composed of good men, but they have neglected their responsibility to these boys.

"We also find that the employees were men who were not

settled in life, who have had no experience in raising boys of their own or any boy and who know nothing about the science of bringing up children."

The superintendent was fired.

Three years later, in 1918, the school was hit with another tragedy when more boys died during a flu epidemic. "Industrial school in critical shape," the Marianna mayor wrote in a telegram to state officials. "Need nurses and doctor, am using every person able, so many cannot attend to all."

The bad news kept coming. Stories about school administrators leasing out students as cheap labor, about loathsome living conditions, about the continued mistreatment of boys.

If anyone was listening, they did little to stop the abuses.

A commission appointed to investigate charges of crowded conditions in Marianna in 1926 found children, some as young as eight years old, "restrained in step chains, which were welded on their ankles."

The public registered its outrage, but again the attention faded. Then things got worse.

Fifteen years later, use of "disciplinary paddling" at the school was officially sanctioned by Governor Spessard Holland and members of his cabinet, all of whom, according to a story in the local paper, were former schoolteachers. The 1941 endorsement was the state's rebuttal of a mother's charge that her son had been whipped bloody by a three-inch board while he was at Marianna. Mullard Davidson, the reform school superintendent at the time, called the claim of brutal treatment "utterly false." The boy had been spanked, not abused, the superintendent said, and even the governor was in favor of a good paddling when it was deserved.

Other newspaper stories documented violence between students on the campus. In 1944, four older boys were accused of beating and strangling a thirteen-year-old because they feared he would report their planned escape from the school. In 1949, one boy fatally stabbed another who threatened to tell that he was smoking on campus.

The new superintendent, Arthur G. Dozier, speaking to the local Exchange Club in 1948, said his school more resembled a college campus than a reformatory for youth.

"If the state of Florida accepts the responsibility for parenthood," Dozier said in his speech, "the least Florida can do is to be a good parent and find for a child the opportunities that have been lacking."

Every year, the school's population grew, up to nine hundred students at one time; conditions worsened, and whispers of vicious beatings got louder. Boys ran away from the school every week. Some were caught by posses and returned. Some were never seen by their classmates again. People who worked at the institution came home with stories about beatings that had gotten dangerously out of control. Some told of boys being killed, their bodies tossed into the Chipola River, or buried in hastily dug graves on school grounds. Parents in town warned their children that if they misbehaved, they would be taken to the reform school and whipped until their skin tore open, like boys up there were.

Time after time, rumors of sanctioned abuse were corroborated by credible eyewitness accounts. In 1958, a Miami psychologist, Eugene Byrd, who had worked for a year at the reform school, testified before a U.S. Senate judiciary subcommittee on juvenile delinquency that boys in Marianna had "a great deal of fear, anxiety and sometimes panic" about being punished. Byrd and another psychologist on staff, "decided we would like to witness this punishment, since it apparently was so meaningful to the boys, and also to corroborate does this actually happen, are the boys' stories actually true," he testified that March before the congressional committee. "So we asked permission from the superintendent of the school to witness this," he said. "Well, this was given after some degree of resistance on his part. But since he did acquiesce, we did watch. It consisted of taking the boys in a group to a small building."

The building, Byrd testified, consisted of two rooms, "one in which they weighed in, the other room in which they are beaten consists of a cot on which they lay down. They are told to hold the head rail and not yell out nor to move. They are beaten by the director of the department, not the superintendent of the school. The superintendent does witness each beating."

Asked to describe the beating, Byrd said, "The blows are very severe. They are dealt with a great deal of force with a full arm swing over his head and down, with a strap, a leather strap approximately a half-inch thick and about 10 inches long with a wooden formed handle. Each boy received a minimum of 15. . . . There was no boy who received less than 15 at that time. . . . There was a very young boy . . . about age 10, who was unable to hold the bed and received approximately 22 lashes."

"What is your opinion?" Senator Estes Kefauver asked the psychologist.

"In my personal opinion, it is brutality," Byrd responded.

Dozier angrily responded that there was no brutality at his school, only "a clash in philosophy."

Florida governor Leroy Collins refused to step in. He said he wouldn't "approve or disapprove" of the practice of whipping boys at Marianna, and that he had told Superintendent Dozier to use his own discretion in disciplining students.

Four months after Byrd's testimony before the Senate subcommittee, in July of 1958, fifteen-year-old Michael Babarsky, who later changed his name to Michael O'McCarthy, was beaten nearly unconscious by Robert W. Hatton, the reform school director and Dozier's right-hand man.

Michael ended up at the reform school after committing a string of minor offenses in his hometown of Islamorada in the Florida Keys. His lapse into juvenile delinquency had been inevitable. Much of Michael's early childhood had been spent tagging along with his stepfather, a brawler named Jim Babarsky who spent nights and weekends in bars with names like The Rusty Nail and The Bucket o' Blood. Jim had told Michael that when he was a boy his stepmother had disciplined him using a hot iron poker. Even though he was a young child, Michael had figured it was that kind of abuse that accounted for his stepfather's Jekyll and Hyde personality. His mother, Edna, didn't care much about Jim's bad temper. "He's a hard worker and a good provider," she said, after one of his violent explosions.

Edna met Jim in the Miami bar where she waitressed. She had left Michael's father to be with him, and Michael rarely saw his father after that. Jim was going places, Edna told her little boy, and they were going with him. Someday he'd make a lot of money and they would all live happily ever after. While Jim was busy building their future, the family lived in a tiny frame house just off of SW 27th Avenue in Miami. As young as Michael was, he doubted the fairy-tale ending his mother predicted.

Most times, when Edna wasn't waiting tables at Small's Shrimp Fry, she didn't get off the couch. She lay there, drowning in a cocktail of whiskey and depression, and Michael tiptoed around her. For a time, at least he had his friend Aubrey to distract him from his muddled home life. Aubrey was the son of a black woman who worked with Edna. They lived on the black side of SW 27th. Usually on afternoons when both mothers were working, Aubrey came to Michael's side of the neighborhood to spend the day.

Aubrey could make a harmonica warble like a songbird and Michael begged to learn to play. One day his friend finally gave in. He blew a note on the harmonica and passed it to Michael for him to do the same. Edna had been dozing on the front porch that afternoon, or so her son thought. But as Michael raised the harmonica to his lips, Edna leapt out of her chair, snatched the instrument out of his hands, and screamed at Aubrey to go the hell home.

That day Edna said the most terrible things that Michael had ever heard her say. For an hour afterward, she raged about "filthy niggers" and their "dark, unclean skin." Even at his tender age—he was in the second or third grade at the time—Michael was sickened by his mother's racist rant. He never saw Aubrey after that, and he bitterly resented his mother for ending their friendship.

It hadn't been a year after that when Jim was offered a job, building a model community of starter homes and multifamily rental units in the Chicago suburb of Park Forest. Michael was around eight at the time. "I told you," his mother had said. "I told you Jim would make something of himself." If making it meant buying a shiny new Packard, a fur coat for Edna, and putting hundred-dollar bills on the kitchen table, then Jim had indeed made it big in Chicago.

Michael got his first real taste of normalcy in the Heartland. After school, he'd ride his bike in the countryside or fish at the nearby creek. It was in Park Forest that he'd learned to bowl, taken his first hayride, dissected his first frog, and had his first girl crush. Sometimes he almost felt happy-go-lucky. But success hadn't quenched Jim and Edna's thirst for copious amounts of liquor, and the late-night sounds of angry voices and breaking dishes continued. Some nights, Michael would see the reflection of the flashing red lights on his bedroom walls, then listen as Jim threatened suicide when the cops dragged him out of the house. The next morning he'd be back, calm and repentant, and Edna would take him back.

After four years in the Midwest, Edna told Michael they were moving back to Florida. Jim had decided to build a big home in Islamorada. Try as he might, Michael just didn't fit in there. At age thirteen, he began looking for ways to fill the emptiness he felt, and he found it in the bottle of Four Roses whiskey his mother kept hidden in the back of a kitchen cabinet.

How Michael loved the warm feeling of the whiskey as it went past his throat and down to his belly. After so many swallows, his self-consciousness dissolved and feelings of giddiness and daring overtook him. It didn't take long before Michael craved the sense of joie de vivre that intoxication brought him. He drank more, and started getting into trouble—skipping school, petty thefts, those kinds of things—often enough that the local sheriff was becoming more fed up with every stunt he pulled. Sometimes the sheriff threatened him, saying, "I'm going to put you away some-day, so help me, boy, I will."

The journey to the White House began simply enough. Michael

had permission from Edna and Jim to have his friend Paul spend the weekend in Islamorada. They were going away, so the boys would have the house to themselves. Michael invited a girl named Dottie to join them and the three guzzled beer. Dottie drank hers through a straw. When all three were stinking drunk, Michael took Dottie to his bedroom where they had clumsy sex. The next thing Michael knew, it was the following morning and a sheriff's officer was standing at his front door.

Dottie had told her parents she was staying with a girlfriend that night, but they found out otherwise and called the authorities to report their daughter missing. Apparently Dottie's friend had divulged her whereabouts.

Do you know where she is? the sheriff asked.

No, Michael lied.

Pushing past him, the sheriff strode into the house and climbed the stairs to the second-floor bedrooms. He found Dottie naked and passed out on Michael's bed. Knowing that his luck had run out, Michel went downstairs and cracked another beer.

Enough was enough, the sheriff said, passing Michael as he whisked Dottie out of the house. "You're going to Marianna."

Michael hated the reform school from the moment he arrived there. He disdained the poor white farm boys who were incarcerated, and he loathed the local yokels who ran the place, men he called "white crackers."

Two months into his sentence, Michael committed the unforgivable act of trying to escape. He and a friend he knew only as Woody had gotten three hours away when they were caught and returned to Marianna.

Their punishment took place in the same building Byrd described in his testimony before the Senate subcommittee, a two-room structure that people on campus called the White House.

Michael was ordered in first. The whip cracked his skin open, and broke his spirit.

When his own beating was over, he was forced to listen from the other room as Hatton took a turn with Woody.

Michael had lost count at fifty lashes, when Woody's screams, finally, mercifully, stopped. He never saw his friend after that, but the sound of Woody's agonized cries would follow him for the rest of his life.

Five years later, in 1963, an anxious thirteen-year-old boy named Robert Straley, willowy and diminutive, took his first trip to the White House on the very day he arrived at the reform school. And there, a one-armed supervisor named Troy Tidwell whipped him senseless. Robert had spent every night for the next two years never knowing when he would be awakened in the middle of the night, accused of some made-up infraction, and taken to the White House to be beaten into delirium.

The only thing worse was the time he was dragged by the one-armed man from his bed to a place the boys called "the rape room" and been so fearful he had fainted without knowing exactly what had happened.

On March 19, 1968, three years after Straley left Marianna, Florida's new governor, Claude Kirk, came calling at the reform school.

By then, Dozier had been promoted in state government and Lenox Williams, a cocky psychologist who had worked at the school for eight years, was named superintendent.

Williams hardly looked the part. His eyes went in opposite

directions, and he drooled residue from the chewing tobacco that was always tucked in his cheek. Williams didn't own a shirt without brown tobacco dribble stains on it.

Kirk, on the other hand, was a self-aggrandizing Republican, a high-living, haughty, publicity hound, who touted his friendship with Richard Nixon, and who was once quoted in *Time* magazine as saying, "This is Claude Kirk, Governor of Florida. Do you read my press? Then you know that I'm a tree-shakin' son of a bitch."

After his tour of Marianna, he was ready to do some tree-shakin'. Kirk fumed at a press conference afterward, "Somebody should have blown the whistle on Marianna a long time ago."

Kirk didn't like Superintendent Williams. He found him to be pompous and disrespectful. He demanded that the living conditions be improved at the reform school. He ordered decrepit buildings razed and renovations for the boys' dormitories, where the beds were so close there was barely room to walk between them, the toilets were backed up, and the walls had holes the size of baseballs.

But what had really troubled him was the attitude of Williams and his staff. When Kirk inspected a dormitory, he noticed that there were no blankets on the beds. Northern Florida could get mighty cold at night, he said to one of his tour guides. "How do these boys keep warm?" he asked Williams.

"Body heat," the man had answered cavalierly.

The obvious poor management of the school pricked at the back of the governor's neck. He put Williams on notice and called for oversight of the school by the new director of the state Division of Youth Services, O. J. Keller.

"The point now is to find funds for repairs, new construction, better personnel and a bigger staff," the *St. Petersburg Times* wrote in an editorial following the governor's visit. "Florida must lift its troubled children from an environment as destructive as Marianna's."

It didn't happen.

The newspaper followed up later that month with a story entitled "Hell's 1,400 Acres." It read, in part:

> Lenox E. "Link" Williams, bulky superintendent of the Florida School for Boys, is frankly worried. The 36-year-old, crew-cut psychologist leans back in his swivel chair and says:
>
> We've never had enough money to staff this facility. We're getting deeper and deeper in the red. As vacancies occur, we don't replace the people who left.
>
> The school, Williams admits, has no real rehabilitation program. It doesn't even have a screening center to separate the hard-core delinquent from the "normal" delinquent, many of whom are at Marianna because they were truant from school.
>
> Asked if boys are learning wrong things, such as crime techniques and sex perversions, Williams blurted: "Hell, yes!"
>
> He adds: "I know some children are harmed by their experience here but what can we do?"

The culture of cruelty kept on, and, less than a year later, on February 3, 1969, Williams was fired. Division of Youth Services director Keller described the reason for his dismissal as twofold: Williams advocated corporal punishment, which Keller opposed, and he had failed to institute Keller's progressive policies.

Williams wasn't going quietly. He denied that he advocated corporal punishment, and that he had continued to authorize beatings even after they were ordered stopped at the school. He filed an appeal, claiming it was "unfair and inequitable to discharge me when I have done nothing more or less than following the instructions which I have received to the best of my ability."

Adding insult to injury, a visit to the facility later that same month by members of the Florida Council of Juvenile Court Judges produced more negative headlines about the reform school. One judge vowed never to send another boy to Marianna. Another was quoted as saying, "When a couple of boys I sent up there came over to say hello I felt like a rat for sending them to that place."

Around the same time, Louis de la Parte, a crusading state legislator from Tampa, paid a surprise visit to the school and found "the blood spattered shed" where boys were beaten. He called the local newspapers. The *Evening Independent* followed up the spate of allegations with a scathing editorial, calling for grand jury intervention. "It is time for a state grand jury to take a look at the Florida School for Boys," the paper wrote on February 25, 1969:

> The only body that could undertake such an investigation would be a grand jury. It would be unburdened by political influence and straightforward in its findings.

Two things happened after that. Wayne Mixon, the Democrat who represented Marianna in the state capital, held a meeting in the town to apologize to residents for the critical remarks made by the judges who had visited the reform school. And Lenox "Link" Williams went before the five-member Career Service Counsel, the politically appointed board charged with hearing his appeal of his termination, and won.

Williams had a friend in Tallahassee, a legislative power-house named Dempsey Barron. People called the Panhandle rancher the most powerful man in Florida politics. Barron had a reputation for clashing with his peers and he rarely lost. Barron famously once directed one governor to "stay the hell out of our business."

The Florida School for Boys was under his authority and he would be the one to make the decisions about who would run it and who wouldn't. Barron didn't have to fight hard to put Williams back in place. The public outcry following the gover-nor's comments a year earlier had died down, and little attention was being paid to the reform school.

Williams was back on the job in May.

If people wondered how an institution so vast, with such pres-ence, just seventy miles from the state capital, could maintain such autonomy, if they wondered why its leaders felt entitled to flay children without fear of reprisal, answers were not forth-coming, at least not publicly.

The fact was that the Florida School for Boys was an indus-try, requiring employment, goods, and services, in an out-of-the-way place, where there was almost no other commerce. People in town needed their jobs. If the boss was a little shady, if things didn't seem quite right, well, you just had to look the other way. There were kids at home to feed.

The combination of economics and isolation allowed the

institution to operate as an independent jurisdiction. And the politicians preferred it that way. Out of sight, out of mind.

A conspiracy of silence.

When Jack Levine, the young teacher from the Bronx, brought back the story of what he had witnessed in Marianna, his bosses in the state capital responded with blank stares. He could hardly believe it.

Levine soon resigned his state job to join the staff of a private child advocacy organization in Tallahassee, but he couldn't get Marianna out of his mind.

Three years after his haunting visit to the reform school, he was contacted by a former Florida public defender named Claudia Wright, asking what he knew about the place. Wright was an outspoken children's advocate who had worked as a pubic defender in Jacksonville between 1978 and 1981. Many of her clients had told her about the terrible things that went on in Marianna. She had left the public defender's office to work for the ACLU's National Prison Project, but only accepted the new position on the condition that she be allowed to investigate Florida's reform schools. Levine said he would be more than happy to help.

The two took a trip to Marianna, arriving, unannounced, on a Sunday afternoon, as Levine had done the first time. Levine had timed the visit to coincide with Superintendent Williams's annual Arkansas fishing trip. The pair managed to get into the isolation building, but they were ordered to leave after about three minutes inside. It had been long enough for Wright to see a small boy hogtied in a cell.

That visit prompted a surprise follow-up by the Inspector General's Office of the Department of Health and Rehabilitative Services, which found that boys as young as ten were being shackled and hogtied at the Florida School for Boys.

Wright and a group of child advocates followed up with a class action lawsuit, which offered a public window into the reform school's claustrophobic culture, and ultimately led to reforms of Florida's juvenile justice system. The suit revealed just how isolated from the outside world the students were, and how completely they were at the mercy of their abusers.

The "cruel and abusive" treatment of students included "restricting their access to and communication with families, the community, and the courts," said the complaint, filed in U.S. District Court on January 1, 1983.

The students were subject to "overcrowding, unsanitary and dangerous physical conditions, lack of security, lack of adequate staff, lack of medical care, abusive punishment, including isolation, hogtying, shackling, and physical abuse, lack of education and programming, lack of due process in disciplinary matters, mail censorship, and deprivation of access to courts."

The staff used "a particularly harmful method [of punishment] called hogtying. They hogtie children by forcing them to lie on their stomachs, handcuffing their wrists behind their backs, shackling their legs together and connecting the handcuffs to the leg shackles.

"Employees have, on many occasions, beaten and kicked children while they were shackled or hogtied.

"[They] leave children locked in isolation cells, lying on concrete beds, sometimes without sheets or mattresses, hogtied or shackled, for extended periods of time."

Even if a child had wanted to reach out to a parent or guardian for help, the school censored all communication with the outside world. Employees opened their mail, and the children were not permitted to send letters in sealed envelopes. Their telephone calls and visits were "improperly restricted."

"[Children] at the reform school have suffered, do suffer, and will continue to suffer immediate and irreparable injury, including physical, psychological and emotional injury," the suit claimed.

"Their intellectual abilities, their emotional health and well-being and their ability to function adequately in the community have seriously deteriorated and will continue to deteriorate" unless the culture of the school changed dramatically, it said.

The lawsuit would eventually drive changes in the state's juvenile justice system. If shining new light on the school could save the system from itself, it was many decades too late for Robert Straley and Michael O'McCarthy and the hundreds, perhaps thousands, of others who had suffered the ravages of the Florida School for Boys.

But it might not be too late for the school's perpetrators to be called to account.

CHAPTER EIGHT

Gus Barreiro was surveying his new office at Florida's Department of Juvenile Justice headquarters in Tallahassee when his cell phone rang. The number of the incoming call was unfamiliar, but he answered anyway.

"This is Gus," he said.

Barreiro was two when he moved with his mother and five-year-old brother from Cuba to Miami, yet his words, forty-eight years later, still carried the hint of a northern Caribbean accent.

"Who is calling?" he asked. "¿Quién está llamando?"

"I'm looking for Gus Barreiro," the man on the other end of the phone said.

"This is Gus Barreiro," he said, rolling his r's slightly.

Michael paused. Weeks earlier, after that first phone call with Robert, he had put the Harriet Tubman project on the shelf and made the Florida School for Boys his priority. Michael had spent hours at his home computer, and on the telephone, searching for ways to get the story into the right bureaucratic hands. There were days he rarely emerged from his office, except to go to the

kitchen for something to eat. Sometimes he didn't acknowledge
Jennifer for a whole day. He was so consumed with his new cause,
and so mired in the personal baggage that came with it, that nothing else mattered. If he could just get someone powerful enough in
state government to acknowledge what happened in Marianna,
he would have done his job. Then he could return to his normal
life.

Couldn't he?

Michael had found Barreiro's name and telephone number
on a Florida child advocacy website. As a state legislator from
Miami, Barreiro had been the go-to person about issues dealing
with children. He had quite a reputation for stepping on toes,
even if they belonged to his fellow Republicans. He was known as
the man who shook the culture of Florida's Department of Juvenile
Justice.

Who better to have on our side? Michael thought.

Michael had never expected to reach Barreiro without considerable effort. He knew how difficult it was to get the attention
of politicians, especially if controversy was involved. He was
stunned when Barreiro picked up.

"Oh, excuse me," Michael said, stammering at first. "I, um,
I didn't expect to get you on the first try."

"What can I do for you?" Barreiro asked.

Michael thought he could like this guy. There was something
in his voice, accessibility you didn't normally find with official
types.

"You have time now?" Michael asked.

"Shoot," Barreiro said.

Michael sat back in his office chair, in his Greenville cottage.
Weeks had passed since he agreed to join Straley in the campaign

to expose the Florida School for Boys and some days he could barely hold it together. At this moment, however, he was Michael O'McCarthy, the zealous social activist, not the wounded boy from Marianna. This is what he did best: fight for justice.

"I have a story to tell you," Michael said, his voice growing stronger.

"I like stories," Barreiro said, sitting down in his swivel chair.

Gus Barreiro was a power broker in Florida politics. Flashy-looking, with a rare combination of olive skin, black hair, and deep blue eyes, he had made a name for himself during his four terms in the Florida legislature. He was known for his theatrics on the House floor, and he tended to be bullish and dramatic when he was trying to persuade his colleagues in Tallahassee to his way of thinking. But he moved mountains.

Critics accused Barreiro of being self-serving and egotistical, certainly a media hound, but most agreed that he had earned his reputation as a tireless crusader for children. He seemed unfazed by his detractors. Perhaps it was his absolute confidence in himself, or maybe he was a bit arrogant. Or was it that he believed so wholeheartedly in his mission? But criticism rolled off him like water from a morning shower. If grandstanding and getting his name in the newspapers could benefit the children of the state, Barreiro would say, then what was to argue?

Barreiro found his calling early, at Mount Senario College in Ladysmith, Wisconsin, where he attended on a football scholarship. As a sophomore, he had written a paper for a criminal justice class about how the government could help troubled boys to find their way. Having been raised without a father, Barreiro thought he knew something about what developing boys needed to become good men. As a youngster, he had been drawn to football as much for the opportunity to bond with men as for the physicality of the sport. He remembered how much it meant to him when a coach patted him on the back and told him he was proud, and how such acceptance from father figures had given him the kind of security he could not get from his mother alone.

The dissertation that launched Barreiro's career was based on the premise that positive reinforcement by male role models went a long way with boys who had reached a turning point in their lives. His professor was so impressed with the term paper that he submitted it for a grant to fund a program for delinquent boys. "Would you consider running it?" he had asked young Barreiro. Barreiro had had a lifelong dream to play professional football, but the professor had planted a seed of thought that germinated, and for weeks afterward he couldn't get the offer out of his head.

At nineteen years old, Barreiro opened the Wisconsin Living and Learning Center, a residential group home for boys with behavior disorders. He stayed for nine years, until a teenager named Bobby Rachels killed himself shortly after being forced to leave the center. Rachels had thrived in Barreiro's care, but he was pulled from the program prematurely when the state funding that had kept him there dried up. News of his suicide was too much for Barreiro. He left Wisconsin and returned to Miami to take a job as codirector of the Dade Marine Institute for Youth.

In working with troubled boys, Barreiro had learned a lot about himself and about the system. Juvenile justice was broken and he wanted to help fix it. He had tried to do it from the inside, but the results were small and slow in coming. The best way to change the system, Barreiro decided, was from a position of power. So he decided to run for political office.

In 1998, Barreiro launched his campaign to run for a state House seat from Miami Beach, and he won. When Republican Party leaders asked the freshman legislator which committee he wanted to serve on, Barreiro chose Juvenile Justice, a committee that got little money and less publicity, a place normally reserved for legislators who were being punished. Nobody else wanted the job. Barreiro quickly made a name for himself, and eventually became chairman of the committee.

When it came to legislation that affected children, party lines blurred for Barreiro. He didn't care if you were from his party, and that included Governor Jeb Bush, or one of the opposing Democrats in the House. He drove a hard bargain to get what he thought was right. He had been in office for under a year when he boldly challenged Bush on proposed legislation that would have imposed stiff punishment for crimes committed with guns. Barreiro thought the punishment was too harsh for young offenders. "Let's keep the kids out of it," Barreiro had argued, but Bush held firm. The legislation would be presented for a vote as it was written, to include juvenile offenders, Bush said.

"Then I'm letting you know I am going to fight you," Barreiro told him.

During the next legislative session, Barreiro, armed with a chart with the pictures and names of every state legislator, went to each member, knelt beside him or her, and quietly made his case. "Will you vote with me?" he had asked each one, checking off names until he had enough votes to take back to the governor. Bush backed off, and Barreiro won an exemption for juveniles. He had stepped on the toes of his boss, and Bush never forgave him.

Barreiro won many admirers along the way, but he also made enemies. In June 2003, a seventeen-year-old boy named Omar Paisley, who was arrested for slashing a neighbor with a sawed-off soda can, died while in custody at the Miami-Dade Juvenile Detention Center. Paisley had been violently sick for two days, retching and moaning, and curled into a fetal position on a dirty cot in a cell he shared with two other boys. And for three days, he lay in his own urine and excrement while officials at the lockup ignored his cries for medical attention.

Barreiro was irate when he heard the story. He pressured the House speaker to appoint a select committee to investigate the Department of Juvenile Justice. Barreiro was named chairman of the committee. Dramatic changes followed at the agency. Three high-ranking administrators were pushed out and eighteen workers were suspended or quit. Barreiro wanted to achieve more to avenge the teenager's death. He called for the dismissal of Bill Bankhead, the politically connected head of the agency. Bankhead took medical leave and never returned. Barreiro lobbied Bush for the job, but Bush chose a New Yorker named Anthony Schembri.

Two years later, in October 2005, Barreiro found himself on one end of a heated exchange with Schembri, who was called before a House committee for questioning about the alleged rape of a mentally disabled teen while in department custody. At one point during the hearing, Paisley's death was raised.

"I'm glad that you brought up Omar Paisley," Schembri said to the panel of legislators. "Because I'll bet that each and every one of you don't know this—do I have everybody's attention here for the moment, please? We have saved eleven Omar Paisleys with appendicitis."

Barreiro exploded.

"You know what?" he said, raising his voice. "I'm going to take offense to that. . . . You know who saved eleven lives? Omar Paisley. Omar Paisley's life saved eleven lives—the one thing Omar Paisley left behind. For the department to take credit, to me, I take offense on behalf of that family, because this committee, because Omar Paisley died the way he died—dogs are treated better than Omar Paisley was treated—that's the reason the department is a watchdog over this."

"I salute you for that," a chastised Schembri replied.

His face bright red, Barreiro spit out his words: "Don't salute me. Don't salute me! But don't salute yourself, either."

Three years after Paisley died, when another boy died while in the custody of the state, Barreiro went to war with the system again. That boy was Martin Lee Anderson, whose death at a Florida boot camp in January of 2006 was caught on videotape. He was the same boy whose story had moved Robert Straley to instigate a crusade to expose the Florida School for Boys.

Barreiro had seen the videotape a month after Anderson died in the admissions area of the Bay County Sheriff's Office Boot Camp in Panama City, in Florida's Panhandle. The video had been shown by the Florida Department of Law Enforcement, which was investigating the boy's death, to a small group of officials, including Barreiro, who was then chair of the House Juvenile Appropriations Committee, and four members of Jeb Bush's staff.

The grainy tape was clear enough for Barreiro to interpret what he saw as a young, black boy "flung around like a rag doll" by five uniformed men who seemed either unaware or uncaring that the boy was in terrible distress. The fourteen-year-old

Anderson had landed at the boot camp after he and four cousins crashed their grandmother's car, which they had taken from a church parking lot during Sunday services to go joyriding. The soundless video of his initiation shows the drill instructors kicking and punching him, when he either will not or cannot obey their orders to run around a running track. At one point, Anderson is on the ground when one guard callously steps over his limp body, kneeing him in the back. Hours later, he was pronounced dead.

Barreiro was sickened by what he saw. He left the room in Tallahassee, where the screening had taken place, and dialed the *Miami Herald*. A front-page story in the next day's paper, written by Carol Marbin Miller, described a "clearly shaken" Barreiro as saying it was "the most heinous treatment of a human being" he had ever witnessed. "He's, like, comatose, and they are punching and punching. This could be anybody's son," Barreiro said. When the reporter contacted the governor's office for comment, a spokesman would only confirm "four people on Bush's staff had viewed the tape, but declined to say what they saw."

The *Herald* story ignited an international media firestorm, and Barreiro used the opportunity to begin a campaign to shut down boot camps across the state. By late April, Barreiro had garnered enough support in the Florida House and the Senate to close juvenile boot camps. Jeb Bush, who had been a strong supporter of the camps, signed the Martin Lee Anderson Act, sealing the deal. It was Barreiro's finest moment, and his political swan song.

After eight years in the Florida legislature, Barreiro had termed out of his office. He was given a standing ovation on his last day on the House floor.

In its May 1, 2006, edition, the *St. Petersburg Times* published a glowing summary of Barreiro's performance in office: "Woven through the political life of state Rep. Gus Barreiro is the subject of death, and how the state's role in the deaths of teenage boys has propelled his relentless quest for change," the story began.

Twenty years ago, when Barreiro ran a home for troubled boys in Wisconsin, a teenager named Bobby Rachels committed suicide after being taken away due to a lack of state funding. Barreiro decided then he wanted to run for public office.

"I wanted Bobby's memory to stand for something," he said.

He returned to Florida and in 1998 won a House seat from Miami Beach. Five years later, another young man's death rocked him. Seventeen-year-old Omar Paisley died of a ruptured appendix at a juvenile lockup in Miami, after spending three days begging for medical attention. A guard told him, "Suck it up."

Then in January, 14-year-old Martin Lee Anderson died after collapsing at a Panama City boot camp. No one in government paid much attention until Barreiro watched a video of guards thrashing the teen. Outraged, he went public, comparing what he saw to the Rodney King beating, "only worse" because Anderson died.

Now, as Barreiro enters the final week of his last legislative session, the term-limited Republican is no longer a lone voice. Boot camps have been eliminated, replaced by a less militaristic program, and the subject of juvenile justice, once a legislative backwater, is a high-profile issue.

"This is a guy who came to Tallahassee to fight for his passion," said Rep. Dan Gelber, D-Miami Beach. "He asked the tough questions over and over and over again. He's shaken the culture of the Department of Juvenile Justice."

Now, Barreiro was working for the same agency he had censured.

Barreiro had been at Juvenile Justice for less than a month when he took Michael's call. He hadn't even had time to hang pictures on his office walls. When his political career ended, two years earlier, he had floundered around, looking for something to do. The new Republican governor, Charlie Crist, had offered him the $72,000-a-year job at DJJ. Barreiro took it believing it would be an opportunity to continue to push his agenda and a way to pay the mortgage. Stirring up controversy so soon, based on a telephone call from a stranger, would be foolhardy.

Still, Barreiro listened intently as Michael described the abuses that took place at the Florida School for Boys. He scribbled notes on a legal pad. *O'McCarthy. Horror stories. Marianna. Torture room. Truth?* The story was so awful it seemed implausible. If what O'McCarthy was saying was true, what went on in Marianna was systematic sadism. It was almost too much to comprehend.

"Listen," Barreiro said, after twenty minutes or so. "What you're telling me is terrible. But I'm not a legislator anymore. I'm at the DJJ. I just started working here." Barreiro felt almost embarrassed by the admission.

Michael was stunned. "I guess you won't be able to help us, then," he said.

"I don't know if I can help," Barreiro said. "I'll do what I can do."

Barreiro hung up the phone and sat in his empty office for a long time, reflecting on the call. He had perceived from the caller's voice the same vulnerability he had heard in the voices of hundreds of boys over the years. Boys who had been tortured and abused in a system that was supposed to protect them, by men who were charged by the state with guiding them.

He never turned his back on a troubled kid.

CHAPTER NINE

Robert and Michael composed their memories of Marianna and posted them on a Web site. Their hope was that the Internet journal would attract others with stories about the reform school. As Michael had said in his first e-mail to Robert, numbers would strengthen their credibility. "There will come a time to share the pain as raw human beings—as survivors of this monstrous legacy of official torture and cruel and inhuman punishment," he wrote. Now, if somehow they could bring attention to their stories, it might embolden other survivors to finally come forward. It would be too easy for people to dismiss as opportunistic, or even a ruse, the claims of two men, Michael said. But how could they brush off ten or twenty men with the same harrowing recollections?

In the inaugural weeks of the crusade, a handful of people e-mailed Robert with their stories. Some had tripped over the Web site while searching on the Internet. Others heard about it from one of the smattering of brief newspaper or television news stories that Robert had finagled with that initial plea to the media—the one that had inadvertently brought him together with Michael. It was Robert's role to monitor the early reaction and he was encouraged by the stories that trickled in. "We're getting somewhere," he reported to Michael in early May, just before heading out on the road for the summer festival tour.

In some of the responses, Robert felt as if he were reading chapters from his own life story. One, from the daughter of a survivor, was particularly painful to confront: "I write this letter with a heavy, heavy heart," Alissa Courtright of Marysville, Ohio, wrote. "I have just learned that my father, while a youth of an undetermined age, was a 'student' at the FSB. My father was no angel by any means, but was in trouble and was sent to the FSB. . . . Growing up, I thought my father was just an unbelievable SOB. I knew he did the best he could, but he was full of rage, had problems with drinking, many other issues. . . . Apparently, my aunt saw a newscast about your group, contacted my father and asked him to contact you, at which he broke down sobbing. My father has cried twice in his life that I remember, and frankly, it has terrified me both times. . . . Looking through this information about the FSB and what he may have gone through there (as he broke down sobbing, I can imagine it was horrific) I am starting to gain a small portion of understanding of the man that is my father and I would appreciate any help you could give me."

Robert's heart ached as he read the woman's words. He wished his own daughter, Rachel—the beautiful girl he had lost to suicide a few years earlier—was still alive so he could tell her about the time he spent in Marianna. If he could, he would tell her how the experience had changed him from a lonely boy into a cynical man and shattered his ability to feel truly connected to anyone. His own catharsis might have helped Rachel to understand his emotional shortcomings, and why he had been able to walk out of her life all those years ago.

Robert had been estranged from Rachel for most of her childhood. Their reconciliation, when she was twenty-four, had been bumpy and uncertain. He had just begun feeling as if he were finally making up for lost time when, in the early spring of 1998, at the age of twenty-six, Rachel killed herself in his home. Ten years later, the pain of her death was still fresh.

Robert's girlfriend and Rachel's mother, a freethinking woman named Marti, were living a hippie's existence in Florida when Marti discovered she was pregnant in 1971. The libertine attitudes of the sixties had been cultivated and, at least in their enlightened circles, the decision to have a child out of wedlock was not just acceptable but au courant. Rachel was born in September of that year. Robert adored his little blonde sidekick. Rachel went where he went. Once she was out of diapers, he even took her with him on the summer tour.

But by the time Rachel was five, his relationship with Marti had run its course and everything changed. For a while, Robert stayed in close contact with his daughter. Then, in March 1980, when Rachel was eight, he met a local woman named Teresa at a B. B. King concert in Tennessee. Teresa wrote her number on a popcorn box; two months later they were married in an elaborate ceremony at the storied Two Rivers Mansion in Nashville. Rachel attended the wedding, but it was Teresa that Robert took on the road with him that summer. At the end of the tour, the newlyweds settled into Teresa's home in Nashville. That same summer, Marti married and moved with Rachel to Michigan. The distance took its toll on Robert. Every minute he would have spent with his daughter, had she been near, he put into his burgeoning business and the elaborate house that he and Teresa were building in the tony Nashville suburb of Goodlettsville. His time with Rachel became less and less frequent and eventually they lost touch. When he saw her again, in 1995, his little girl was all grown up.

Rachel had called Robert out of the blue that year. She was twenty-four and living in Ohio with her young son, Jake. A struggling singer, she had made it as far as the stage at Radio City Music Hall before she got pregnant and followed her boyfriend to the Midwest to live. Stage work was hard to come by in Columbus, Rachel said to Robert, and she was stuck living in a bad neighborhood because money was tight. Robert seized on his daughter's despair as an opportunity to make up for his long absence from her life. "If you're willing to come to Nashville," he said, "you'll have everything you need." A week later, Robert was driving to Columbus in a U-Haul truck, ready to move his daughter and three-year-old grandson to Tennessee.

By then, Robert's marriage to Teresa was fifteen years old and faltering. He lavished all his attention on Rachel, renting her an apartment near his home and filling it with expensive new furniture. He bought her a shiny new Ford Taurus and doled out a weekly allowance for gas. Rachel tried to fill the hole in her heart with material things, and things were all that Robert knew how to give, but it was never enough to heal the guilt he felt for abandoning her. Rachel's forgiveness had seemed unconditional and, ultimately, it was tragically fleeting.

In April 1998, Robert was in Florida, preparing to sell the house his mother had bequeathed him in her will, when a neighbor from Nashville called to say that there had been a terrible accident.

"It's Rachel," the woman said.

"Is she all right?" Robert asked.

"She's been shot."

"By whom?" Robert asked.

"She shot herself, Robert," the woman said, breaking down in tears. "And she's dead."

Robert drove all night back to Tennessee. The sun was rising when he pulled up to his home. Yellow police tape blocked the front door, but he went inside anyway. Robert and Teresa had recently divorced and he figured that Rachel had chosen to take her life in his house because no one was there. Her body had been taken to the city morgue by then, but the spot where she died was evident. On the floor, next to Robert's desk, lay two quilts. Rachel had put the quilts down so as not to stain the carpet with her blood. She had said as much in her suicide note, which Robert would later read.

The detective investigating Rachel's death told Robert that she had shot herself in the stomach. That was common for women, he said. They were usually too vain to disfigure their own faces. Since the inquest had not yet been officially closed, Robert wasn't allowed to see the body. He would be asked at the city morgue to identify Rachel through a photograph taken postmortem. Robert went white when he looked at the image of his dead daughter. Rachel was barely recognizable, her face had so distorted in death. Her mouth was gaping open, presumably frozen that way as she gasped her last breath.

Clutching the picture in his hand, he closed his eyes and flashed back to the little, blond girl seated next to him in his van. He is driving to the next town on the summer tour and she is chattering and giggling about a circus act she just saw. Robert had tried to freeze the image in his consciousness as he stood there, holding the grotesque image of his only child. Letting his little girl go had been the worst decision of his life. He had been so distracted by a new wife and a growing business that Rachel had just slipped out of his mind. Then she was gone again, but this time for good, and unremitting remorse had taken her place.

Robert had handed the photograph back to the morgue attendant and signed his name on the dotted line. Three days later, he took the urn with Rachel's ashes to Mount Olivet Cemetery in Nashville, where they used to go together to admire the statuary. He placed the ashes in the marble hands of his favorite angel. It was shortly afterward when he discovered a poem Rachel had written. "What they will never understand," it said, "is that forgiveness is only for the strong." For the rest of his life, Robert would wonder if the poem was meant for him. He would also mourn the relationship he might have had with his grandson, Jake, who went to live with his father.

Facing his past had come too late to spare the pain that Robert had passed on to Rachel and everyone else he ever loved. His atonement would be in trying to help keep others from living in the grip of gut-wrenching regret, as he did.

Robert composed himself after reading the letter from Alissa Courtright, and then he contacted her and urged her to begin a dialogue with her father before it was too late for them, too. Ask him questions, Robert said. Don't take no for an answer. A few days later, she wrote again to say that she had taken his advice:

"Robert, I spoke to my father last night, at length, about his experiences there at FSB. While shock and horror can't accurately describe my reaction to his words, I am thankful to know my father better. I want to thank you and the others for that. Without your strength and courage, these conversations would have never happened in his life and I would be left wondering who my father was. . . . I want to help you and the men like my father. If there is anything that I can do, if you need someone to help research, investigate, anything, please, reach out to me. My background in college is in Psychology and Sociology, with several years of working with the sexually abused. I don't know what use you may have for me, but I'd like to do something. I want to help you and the men like my father."

Marianna's sweep had been wide and it was overwhelming. For every boy who had been victimized, it was likely that a family had suffered the collateral damage. If healing was possible, it could only begin with acknowledgment and truth from the people who had lived it. For all of the historical testimony about the sins of Marianna, the victims had never spoken out. They would need to bear witness if there was any chance to get justice for all who had suffered, Robert thought, and to stop history from repeating itself yet again.

Timothy McCarty, an inmate in a South Carolina prison, wrote of his "nightmare" while he was at the school in 1958. He entered the school when he was fifteen, and wrote about being beaten by Hatton and Tidwell. "When I was released from there in December 1958, I was a very bitter, angry young man filled with hate. . . . I'm not going to blame all of my bad behavior and law breaking on my horrible experience in Marianna, but I'd be lying if I said I didn't believe that it contributed. . . ."

There but for the grace of God go I, Robert thought when he read the letter. Robert had been sixteen, and had been liberated from Marianna a year earlier, when he was sentenced to five years of hard labor for stealing tires. At the time, he had gotten tangled up with his best friend from the reform school—a boy who had earned Robert's undying loyalty because he had taken a beating for him at the White House. When the friend suggested they steal a set of tires and sell them for spending money, Robert had gone along. As they fled from the station, though, someone had jotted down Robert's license plate number and the police quickly closed in. He was sent to Apalachicola Correctional Institute where the hard labor consisted of loading hot bricks, fresh from the kilns, up onto a flatbed trailer. Pitching hot bricks was nothing compared to the punishment he had endured at Marianna. He served two and a half years, and, in an unfortunate twist of fate, returned to his hometown of Clearwater and immediately found himself in more trouble.

Robert met up with another friend he had met at Marianna. The boy asked if he wanted a ride. Robert had barely settled into the passenger seat when the cops roared up. Unbeknownst to Robert, his friend was driving a stolen car. Robert spent the next two years in a Florida road camp. At the conclusion of his sentence, the captain of the camp called Robert into his office, sat him down in a chair, and meted out the best advice Robert had ever been given: "The reason you are in here to begin with is because of your relationship with your mother," Robert remembered Captain Hinson telling him. "That's where all of your troubles began. I'm not saying you shouldn't visit her, but at least live in a different town and leave your friends behind because they will only get you into more trouble. You're free, you're white, and you're twenty-one. Now go to work and make a life for yourself." Robert had never looked back.

Perhaps if Timothy McCarty had had a Captain Hinson in his

life, things would have been different for him. How many boys from Marianna had grown into angry men, Robert wondered. Dozens? Hundreds? How many had turned their rage inward, or directed it at society, or their wives and children, rather than face down their childhood demons? How many generations of families had been ruined because a small group of twisted men had taken advantage of their power and tainted legions of powerless boys over several decades?

How many men like Willie Hayes were out there, still afraid of the dark some fifty years after their Marianna nightmare ended? Robert read his story through tears.

"One must remember that for me to sit down and try to resurrect old memories that I have buried deep in the back of my mind for over fifty years is very painful, so some of my recollections of exact times and places may not be as accurate as I would like; however, many of my recollections will always be embedded in my mind because they come back from time to time in the form of horrible nightmares," Hayes wrote.

"Mr. Hatton and Mr. Tidwell were on each side of me and Mr. Tidwell held me by my arm. . . . When we arrived at the White House Mr. Hatton unlocked the door at one end of the building and said get your ass in there boy and shoved me. It was about a 6-inch step up and I stumbled as he shoved me in the door and we were in a hallway with rooms on each side. The stench of that building was so bad I began to gag and vomit from being scared and the smell of the place. I was shoved into a room I think on the left and then shoved onto a bed where I was told to get face down on the bed. I was then told to hold onto the rail at the head of the bed and face the wall. I was told that if I tried to get up or if I looked at them they would stop and start all over again. At this time one of them turned on what sounded like a big blower apparently to muffle the sounds of the beating and crying.

"No matter how many stories you hear about this place I don't think anything in the world could prepare you for what was about to happen next. As I lay there waiting I heard the sound of a shoe turning on the concrete floor and then it happened. The worst pain I have ever experienced in my life. I received 45 licks on my buttocks and just before each lick I could hear that shoe pivot on the concrete floor from the sand on the floor. When Mr. Hatton finally quit beating me, I was told to get my ass up and let's go. When we got to the door to go out of the White House I could not make the 6 inch step down to the ground because my buttocks was so numb and I could not tell how much damage was done to them, I could feel blood running down my legs but I was too afraid to say anything. . . . My buttocks was as black as a crow and bloody. I had pieces of my under shorts embedded in my skin and I tried to pull as much as I could out but it hurt too bad to touch. . . . That was my first time to go to the White House but surely not my last.

"Several months later . . . I was awakened in my bed and I was told I was going down if I didn't tell them who had some cigarettes in our dorm. I told him I didn't know who had the cigarettes and he took me by the arm and led me out of the dorm, and we were headed in the direction of the school house. When we got to the side of the school there was a room that led down stairs. I had never been there before but I had been told that was where they would take you and rape you or kill you. This place looked like it was a cellar or something. When we got to the top steps there were two other men there and I didn't recognize the other men. As we approached the top step to go down I started to fight and try to get out of the guard's mighty grip and the two other men tried to help subdue me but I was fighting and screaming for all I was worth, I was kicking at their groin and knee area and swinging my fists at anything I could hit. At one moment I was free from the guard's grip and I started running for all I was worth. I ran for what seemed like forever and my buttocks was beginning to bleed from the beating I had received a few days earlier. I continued to run into some woods until I could not hear them and I thought they had given up on me."

How Robert wished that he had run when he was taken down to the rape room, he thought, reading Willie's story. The misery of that encounter—as he lay there shuddering in the darkness, anticipating his attackers' next moves—had been buried deeper than all the other terrifying memories of Marianna, but not deep enough. If Robert took himself back to that night, and he tried desperately not to, he could still feel the weight of the man's bulky body pressing into his frail frame, hear his grunts, smell his foul breath. He would get trapped in the memory until he finally made himself scream to break free from it.

Willie had escaped the rape room, but Hatton and Tidwell hadn't given up on finding him. After a day on the run, he was captured by two locals and held until Hatton and Tidwell could get to town to retrieve him. Then he was returned to the White House and given one hundred licks with the whip. "Mr. Tidwell did the beating that time," Willie wrote.

"I feel in my heart that God must have a special seat in Hell for people like R. W. Hatton, Troy Tidwell, Arthur Dozier and others like them," he wrote.

"I can remember on a few occasions boys would go to the White House and never return to their cottage. . . . So what happened to them? Where are their bones buried? How many of them had no family at home to question the authorities?

"I suddenly find myself sitting here crying like a 65 year old child, like I said I am resurrecting old memories that I have had suppressed for over 50 years and its getting to me so I will end for now and try to replace these old memories back in their place in the back of my memory bank. Maybe one day we can have a Marianna reunion and all have a good cry and then celebrate our survival together. So long for now, Willie"

They were evil men, indeed, Robert thought, Hatton and Tidwell and the others who had exploited helpless boys. Had they lived out their lives without remorse? he wondered. Or had they been regretful and carried the guilt to their graves? Surely they were dead by now. Or were they? He had to find out.

In a letter to a national child advocate with whom he had begun corresponding, Robert wrote,

"Dear Isabelle: We are really getting somewhere with our effort. . . . We have seven victims that have agreed to write in detail their account of their whippings at the Florida School for Boys now the Arthur G. Dozier School for Boys . . .

"We have enough historical proof," he said, "and enough credible victims to go forward."

CHAPTER TEN

The student nicknamed Blackie had a way about him. Maybe it was his easy smile, or maybe it was that his bigness belied the gentleness of his nature. Whatever it was, Dutch Rowe took a liking to the boy the very first time they met in the carpentry shop at the Florida School for Boys.

Dutch was a small, wiry man with intoxicating blue eyes and a soft spot for children. He had six of his own, two boys and four girls. Dutch had been hired to work on the grounds crew at the reform school, but was quickly promoted to the carpentry shop because of his woodworking ability. He considered himself lucky to nab a job at the school. Jobs were scarce in rural Jackson County, and the ones at the school were especially hard to come by because nearly everyone wanted them. Had it not been for his work there, Dutch might have been laboring under the withering Southern sun in some farmer's field, picking cotton or peanuts, or gathering corn to be able to support his considerable family. At Marianna, he started work early in the morning and arrived home in time to tend his vegetable patch before supper was served.

There were always boys assigned to help Dutch in the carpentry shop, and he was kind to all of them. Even before he started working there, when the school siren wailed at night, signaling that a boy escaped, Dutch had his wife, Allie, prepare a plate of food, then he'd walk it outside and place it on the shelf that held the bucket for the well. The Rowes lived in the rural settlement of Kynesville, up the road a piece from Marianna. Runaways often fled by way of the creek that ran behind the reform school, so the search dogs would have a tougher time picking up their scent. The same creek trickled past the Rowes' farmhouse in Kynesville.

"I know you're out there," Dutch would call out into the empty night, as he carried a plate of rice and beans with collards or cabbage, corn bread and biscuits, and a pork chop or slice of ham to the well—unless it was Sunday; then it would be freshly killed chicken from the barnyard.

"There's food here for you. I'm leaving it."

Then Dutch would walk back into the house to reassure his frightened children that the boys from the school wouldn't hurt them, and whoever it was that had escaped would take the food and be on his way. As sure as Dutch had said it, only the empty plate was there in the morning.

"Those boys got themselves in a little trouble, that's all," Dutch told his children. "They're not bad kids, really."

Dutch liked all the boys who came through the carpentry shop, but the only one he ever mentioned by name was Blackie. In the 1950s in the South, it wasn't every white man who would take a delinquent black kid under his wing, but Dutch believed that all people deserved a chance in life, and Blackie hadn't had much of one. As Dutch told it, Blackie came from a troubled home somewhere in rural Florida. He was sentenced to Marianna for some minor teenage peccadillo, joyriding in a relative's car, or truancy, Dutch couldn't remember exactly what. Yet Blackie had been at the school longer than almost any other student, because every time he was due to leave he did something punishable so he would have to stay. Dutch figured that Blackie had no place else to go. At least at the reform school he had a bed and three meals a day. Didn't matter if the mattress was hard and the food was tasteless if you had nothing to compare it with.

So Dutch did what he could for Blackie. Sometimes he shared the lunch he had brought from home rather than watch the boy eat the mush that came out of the cafeteria. When he could, he gave Blackie the plum assignments in the carpentry shop, and none was more coveted than working on the school's outdoor Christmas display. From Thanksgiving through Christmas, people came from miles around to see the animated holiday extravaganza on the sloping lawn of the Florida School for Boys. Dutch took pride in taking his own children to see it. Every year, the carpentry shop produced a new character—an elf or a reindeer or a cartoon figure—to add to the production. Day and night, people spilled from the cars that lined both sides of the street alongside the school campus, marveling at the exhibition. It was Marianna's Disneyland.

Martha Bennett was home alone in Palatka when she heard the teaser for the local TV newscast. Coming up at eleven. Florida Reform School Abuse Victims Recall Horrors. Martha dropped what she was doing and set her alarm clock to make sure she was awake for the late-night broadcast. Even as she set her clock, Martha knew what she would hear. After all these years, she said to herself, someone is finally coming forward.

Dutch's daughter still thought about that day when her father came home from work with the awful news about Blackie. She was ten at the time. Now she was sixty-six. Martha had long since left the Marianna area and only went back occasionally to visit relatives who still lived there. At the age of nineteen, she had married a local man named Fred Bennett and moved 260 miles southeast to Palatka, where Fred got a job as a wildlife officer. Martha stayed at home to raise their two daughters and, once they were grown, she went to work for the county judge. The Bennetts had a good life in Palatka. Then, in 2000, Fred died of a heart attack and left Martha a widow. Four years later, she retired from her job. For years, she had worked for the presiding judge in the county. These days, she spent most of her time looking after her two teenage grandchildren while their parents worked.

Dutch had died the year after Martha moved away from home. He had never spoken of Blackie again after that day he came home from the reform school, ashen-faced, and told his family that his favorite student had been savagely killed.

According to Dutch, he hadn't seen Blackie for a day or two. When he asked after him, one of the other employees told him that the boy had tried to run away—it must have been almost time for him to be released. This time, when the guards caught wind of his plan, they had had enough. They took Blackie to a small wooden bridge on the Ecofina Creek and beat his head with a railroad spike. They left the spike in the wood of the bridge.

Martha watched Channel 12 that night. She didn't need to be awakened by the alarm clock. She could hardly wait for the newscast to begin. The story, which had emanated from Robert Straley's e-mail to the media, the same one that had found its way to Michael O'McCarthy, told the story of alleged atrocities and possibly even murders that had taken place at the Florida School for Boys during the 1950s and 1960s. At the end of the broadcast, an e-mail address was shown so that others with stories of Marianna might come forward. The e-mail address was Robert's. Martha clicked off the TV, turned on her computer, and started writing.

"I believe your story is every word the truth," she wrote. "I lived in Marianna until 1961. I grew up just a short distance from the reform school. My father worked there periodically and would tell us things that happened there, but like so many outsiders, we thought he was telling us this almost like a scare tactic so that we would not misbehave. . . . I trust and encourage you to seek justice for the young boys that were murdered there. God bless you and may God use his healing powers to heal you and the others by having the liberty to finally discuss and unveil this tragedy."

It wasn't until Robert followed up the e-mail with a telephone call that Martha felt emancipated from her own pent-up memories.

"There was a boy named Blackie," she said. "I never will forget . . ."

Robert and Martha talked for long time that day. When the conversation ended, they promised to stay in touch, and then Robert dialed Michael in Greenville to tell him the story.

"I wonder how many Blackies there were," Robert said.

"There's just no telling," Michael replied. "That's why we have to keep going with this. We have to do it for the boys who can't tell their stories."

The snowball that had begun with a single, local news broadcast was about to turn into an avalanche.

CHAPTER ELEVEN

Gus Barreiro didn't fit in at Florida's Department of Juvenile Justice. Most of the administrators in the office were career bureaucrats and they resented him for his role in shaking up the department a few years earlier. Word had gotten around that the maverick newcomer lobbied Governor Charlie Crist for the top spot at DJJ, but was trumped by the more compliant Frank Peterman, a Baptist minister from St. Petersburg who gave up his legislative seat to take the job. Barreiro liked the African-American Democrat, but he had been surprised by the choice because Crist and members of the selection committee indicated that the job would be his if he wanted it. When Peterman offered him the secondary position, he had accepted with reservations.

DJJ was cliquish, and Barreiro was viewed as a gate-crasher. Even as a legislator and chairman of the Juvenile Justice Committee, he had been invited only twice to walk the halls of the department, and it was clear then that he was thought of as an adversary. On his first day of work there, he had felt a sense of excitement when he swiped his access badge and marched through the department's doors to his new position. He was confident that, if nothing else, he could help the agency regain its footing with his friends in the Florida legislature, both Republicans and Democrats, and he was eager to get to it. Instead, during those first few difficult weeks, he was given busy work and all but ignored. It seemed as if the higher-ups didn't know what to do with him.

Barreiro's office was halfway down a long hallway of offices on the second floor of the sprawling juvenile justice complex. His coworkers passed by without so much as a glance, never mind a cordial hello. Some seemed to go out of their way to avoid him. Two colleagues had been brazen enough—or angry enough—to tell him that he'd never be accepted as one of them. In House committee meetings, he had laid the agency bare too many times and people blamed him for the department's bad name. Barreiro was thick-skinned, but he wasn't accustomed to being frozen out or, even worse, being idle.

One of his first meetings as an employee of the agency had been a real eye-opener for Barreiro. A colleague who had been there for more than two decades introduced herself to a group of child service providers as "part of the B club." The B club, she proudly explained, consisted of people who worked for the agency before the sitting administration took office and who aimed to be there long after Crist and his team left. Barreiro was stunned by her candor. The collective mind-set of the B club seemed to be job survival. What happened to helping kids? he wondered.

After nearly a month in the department, Barreiro still wasn't sure what his job was, and he was restless. But two days after he took the call from Michael O'McCarthy, he was visited by Assistant Secretary Rex Uberman and finally given his marching orders. Barreiro's assignment was to oversee the state's residential programs. His first task, Uberman said, would be to visit the Arthur G. Dozier School for Boys—the former Florida School for Boys. There were problems at Marianna, Uberman said, reports of violence among the students and abusive treatment by guards.

One of the most troubling reports involved a teenager named Justin Caldwell. His father had written the FBI, claiming that his son was being mentally and physically abused at the reform school: "While at Dozier he has had his face smashed into a door by a staff member who also threatened to kill him twice," Mark Caldwell wrote. "My son has been 'choked out' which means choked from behind until he loses consciousness so many times he does not remember. He has witnessed the abuse of other juveniles as well, and approx 3 weeks ago he had his head banged repeatedly on a concrete floor on 2 different occasions the 2nd of which he had to go to Jackson county hospital for a Cat Scan because he lost consciousness. . . . There are too many incidents of abuse to write about, you need to talk to Justin Caldwell and the other youth at Dozier. My son and the other youth at Dozier are supposed to receive help and this is abuse instead and it is criminal to treat our children this way!"

The department needed to get to the bottom of what was going on at the school, Uberman said. There were too many complaints of things going wrong. Barreiro thought it a strange quirk of fate that the reform school had come to his attention twice in one week. He also suspected that his bosses at DJJ were trying to get him out of the office. That was all right by him. He went home, packed a bag, and drove to Marianna that same afternoon.

The last rehabilitation of Marianna had been ordered by Consent Decree and approved by the United States District Court on July 7, 1987. The crackdown was the consequence of the Bobby M. class action lawsuit, which had been brought by child advocates after Jack Levine found the boy hogtied in an isolation cell. The highly publicized case of *Bobby M. v. the State of Florida* had settled on the eve of trial, saving the state further embarrassment over the way it dealt with children in state custody. The agreement had been bartered by Albert J. Hadeed, a no-nonsense attorney with the Southern Legal Counsel, who took a no-holds-barred approach to negotiations with the state. "Settle," Hadeed had threatened the opposition, "or I'll release every horror story I have in my possession to the press."

The consent decree, approved by District Court Judge Maurice M. Paul, set forth sweeping reforms in Florida's juvenile justice system. Children at Marianna and the state's two other juvenile facilities would no longer be subject to corporal punishment, nor could they be placed in isolation, the agreement said. Children who were thirteen and younger would be removed from the training schools, and the rest would get better access to education, legal and psychological counseling, and their families. By signing the consent decree, the state conceded that it failed its institutionalized children and pledged that children in state care would no longer be treated like wild animals. It was considered a huge victory for Florida's incarcerated children.

"These reforms launch Florida into a new and progressive era," said Gregory Coler, the secretary of the Department of Health and Rehabilitative Services, in a veiled attempt to spin the story away from the muddled bureaucracy that had allowed the abuse of children for so long.

Judge Paul assigned a well-known child advocacy attorney from New Jersey to monitor Marianna's progress. Paul DeMuro had his work cut out for him. By the time he arrived at the reform school, Link Williams, the imperious superintendent, had been transferred to a menial state job until he could be eligible for retirement, but the autonomous culture that had swelled under his leadership would be harder to get rid of.

DeMuro worked alongside the newly appointed superintendent, a man named Roy McKay, Williams's erstwhile assistant. McKay was a solid guy, but DeMuro wondered whether he, like many superintendents before him, had gotten the job through political patronage rather than stellar credentials or an altruistic obligation to save the state's youth. McKay lived in town and many of his neighbors worked at the reform school. Rather than fire those friends and acquaintances with a proclivity to abuse students, McKay transferred them to jobs where their exposure to the boys was limited. Better that, he decided, than to incur the wrath of the community. With DeMuro monitoring the operation, hogtying and torturous isolation was quickly eliminated, but cracking the culture of cruelty proved more challenging, especially because the people who had practiced systematic abuse under Williams were still on the payroll.

Change is driven by power, whether it emanates from a charismatic leader or the wrath of an angry public. The Bobby M. case had sparked the first real effort in decades toward overhauling the state's juvenile justice system. The public outcry over the way children were being treated in state institutions was fierce, and politicians had at least given lip service to the idea of reform, promising more funding and better training. After months of monitoring the reform school, DeMuro began to see a flicker of hope that the system was on the cusp of reform. At Marianna, population caps were being enforced, helping to eliminate overcrowding; the living cottages, which had been in a sorry state of repair, were retrofitted with modern fixtures; and psychological services for students were increased. They were fundamental changes, and it was a start. In a report to Tallahassee, DeMuro wrote that although there was still a long row to hoe, he was "encouraged." Then something happened that blew the possibilities to bits.

On September 14, 1993, a group of teenagers approached a car with two sleeping British tourists at a rest stop on Interstate 10, thirty-five miles east of Tallahassee. The teens knocked on the car window, awakening thirty-four-year-old Gary Colley and his longtime partner, thirty-seven-year-old Margaret Jagger. The couple had spent a few days in New Orleans and were headed to St. Petersburg to visit friends. Tired from the long drive, they had pulled into the rest stop at around 2:00 a.m. to take a short nap before driving the second half of the ten-hour trip. When the teens demanded money, Colley threw the car into gear and attempted to drive away. The teenagers opened fire, killing Colley and injuring his girlfriend.

A publicized transcript of the woman's frantic 911 call was chilling:

"This is the nine-one-one operator. What is the emergency?"

"I want an ambulance," Jagger cried frantically. "My husband's dying. We've been shot. We're at Monticello rest area on Interstate 10. . . . I'm waiting for an ambulance. He's dying. He's really dying. . . . Please hurry. . . . We've been shot. . . . And there is blood all coming out of his mouth and I think he's dying."

The story generated headlines around the world and shook

Florida's $30 billion tourism industry. And suddenly, the benevolence of Florida's legislature toward troubled youth withered.

Barreiro checked into the Marriott, just off the I-10 exit to Marianna, then drove to the reform school to take a look. Parking his car on the shoulder of South Street, he peered through the barbed-wire fencing that enclosed the property. The campus was isolated and it was sprawling, much larger than he had imagined, and it had a softball field and a swimming pool. Yet there wasn't a child in sight. Not a single kid outside, enjoying the grounds. How strange, he thought. Barreiro sat there in his car for a while. His mind wandered to the telephone call from Michael O'McCarthy, and he found himself wondering what was going on inside the brick-and-concrete buildings clustered at the crest of the hilly campus. One was a simple, white structure that fit the description of the place O'McCarthy had said boys were taken and tortured, sometimes for no reason at all, a place O'McCarthy had referred to as the White House. Barreiro decided he'd ask about it in the morning, after he'd introduced himself to the staff. But before he did anything else, he needed to get a haircut.

The local barber was friendly enough.

"What are you doing in town? he asked Barreiro.

"I'm here from Tallahassee," Barreiro said, "visiting the Dozier school."

The ears of the man in the next chair perked up. "Oh yeah, that's been here for years," he said.

"What's the history?" Barreiro asked.

"They used to hurt boys out there," a second customer said.

"Tell me more," Barreiro said.

The men were more than willing to talk. They said that everyone in town had either worked at the reform school or knew someone who worked there. Everyone had heard stories of terrible beatings that had sometimes gotten out of hand, and whispers of boys who had died at the hands of overzealous guards. People gossiped about what went on, but no one had ever wanted to get involved. What could they do? The reform school had been like an all-powerful sovereign state.

Barreiro was stunned. Kids had been tortured, perhaps even killed, and it was common knowledge in Marianna, yet no one had done anything to try to stop it. He was reminded of Nuremberg, Germany, where the townspeople pretended not to notice as the fledgling Nazi Party set down roots in their midst. As far as Barreiro was concerned, if the stories were true, the town was complicit in the crimes that had been committed against children at the school.

Barreiro hardly slept that night. He arrived at the reform school early the next morning with one thing on his mind.

"What do you know about this place that was called the White House?" he casually asked Milton Mooneyham, the assistant superintendent.

Mooneyham was a gentle man. A husband and father of two grown children, he had started at the reform school thirty-nine years ago as a teacher after graduating from Florida State University. He knew all about the White House, he told Barreiro. They used to beat boys there, he said, but not anymore. The building was still there, although no longer in use, he said. Did Barreiro want to see it?

"Sure," Barreiro said.

With Mooneyham leading the way, the two walked to the same white building that Barreiro had spotted from the road the day before. The door was padlocked.

"Can we get the keys?" Barreiro asked.

Absolutely, Mooneyham said.

Mooneyham called his office and had the keys delivered. Unhinging the padlock, he pushed open the door to the small, whitewashed building. The door creaked, the same way doors in horror films always did, Barreiro thought. Barreiro followed Mooneyham into the tiny building.

What he saw reminded him of an old jail—the kind you saw in westerns. The place was dingy and crumbling from neglect, and it was obvious that it hadn't been used for quite some time.

Barreiro looked around, imagining how frightened boys must have been when they were brought there. He recalled O'McCarthy's story, about being ordered down on the dirty mattress and hearing the whoosh of the whip as it bore down on him, and how he welcomed the moment when darkness would finally descend upon him and he could no longer feel the flesh of his back and his buttocks tearing open. Standing there, inside that dingy building, Barreiro could almost hear the screams of the children as the whip cut into their skin. He suddenly felt sick.

"I've seen enough," he said.

Back in Mooneyham's office, a secretary mentioned that there were records with the names of all the boys who had ever been at the reform school. They were stored in a room right down the hall, she said.

"Show me," Barreiro said.

Ledgers by the dozen lined the archive walls. Barreiro took one of the books from the shelf and began leafing through it, then a second, and a third. The names of hundreds of boys spilled from yellowed pages. Some had been as young as five and six years old when they were admitted to the reform school. Barreiro was overcome with emotion as he read the names. One caught him completely off guard: There, in old-fashioned cursive was the name "Michael Babarsky." Inmate number 27719. Son of A. J. and Edna Babarsky of Islamorada. Sentenced by Judge Eva Gibson for stealing and running away "until legally discharged." Admitted on May 14, 1958. Escaped July 7, 1958. Recaptured the next day. Barreiro remembered Michael telling him that his birth name was Babarsky, and that he came from Islamorada. So, there it was, Barreiro thought, in all its dispassionate detail. "How many boys suffered?" he wondered. "How many boys died?"

Barreiro finished out the week in Marianna and returned to Tallahassee exhausted. After a sleepless weekend, he returned to his office at DJJ and shut himself inside. He finally had a mission, but it had little to do with his assignment from Rex Uberman. Barreiro picked up the phone and dialed the number that was scribbled on the notepad in front of him. He knew the call would mean the beginning of the end of his career at the agency.

Michael O'McCarthy answered his cell phone on the first ring. He hadn't expected to hear back from Barreiro, especially not so soon. Barreiro got straight to the point.

"Okay, Mike, you got me," he said, his voice quavering. "What do we do now?"

CHAPTER TWELVE

Carol Marbin Miller was a tough-as-nails beat reporter who was as feared as she was revered by Florida power brokers. In her eight years at the *Miami Herald* and before that the *St. Petersburg Times,* the erudite journalist had upended careers with her hard-hitting stories about the inefficiencies and missteps of the state's notoriously inept child welfare system, and bureaucrats on the wrong side of right shivered when they heard she was on the line.

She had made a sport out of elbowing the status quo, and her portfolio was an impressive collection of page-one stories that had changed the way Florida's social service agencies did business. A twenty-five-year veteran of Florida newspapers, she knew where all the bodies were buried within the state bureaucracy. And her Rolodex was crammed with the names of loyal sources.

Marbin Miller was only nineteen when she backed into the news business. An African-American insurance salesman named Arthur McDuffie had died after a high-speed chase with the Miami police that year. Witnesses claimed the officers had beaten

McDuffie to death after he surrendered, but the police claimed his injuries resulted from a fall from his motorcycle. An investigation suggested that the officers had lied. Not only had they beaten McDuffie to death, but they rolled their squad cars over his body to make it look like he had been in a traffic accident. Six officers went on trial and several eyewitnesses, including three officers who had been at the scene that day, testified against them. One of the witnesses described the officers as having acted like "a pack of wild dogs attacking a piece of meat." The Dade County medical examiner testified that the brain damage that had been inflicted by the beating was the worst he had ever seen. Yet the jury, which consisted of six white men, found the officers not guilty. The reaction to the verdict was fierce and fast. Miami erupted in deadly violence that lasted several days, and the National Guard was called in to restore order.

Marbin Miller's father had driven her to the airport on one of those days, so she could catch a flight back to college in Tallahassee. On the drive through the city, the sight of armed national guardsmen on every corner had transfixed her. She'd never seen anything like it. Back at Florida State University, she pounded out an essay about the experience and submitted it to the college paper. The editor published it. That moment was an the epiphany for her, and it became clear that she wanted to be a journalist. She went on to earn a master's degree at Columbia Journalism School and never looked back.

With her self-deprecating humor, Marbin Miller liked to say that it wasn't any particular talent that made her the best at what she did; it was the fact that she enjoyed shaming people into doing the right thing. When Marbin Miller reported that a state agency had spent thousands of dollars on a court fight to deny a twelve-year-old blind boy with cerebral palsy the special thermal blankets he needed, Governor-elect Charlie Crist wrote a personal check to the boy to cover the cost of a year's worth of the blankets. The agency's director resigned the next day. When a child advocate called her with a tip about a child who had been taken off an organ transplant list because he was disabled and in foster care, Marbin Miller wrote the front-page story, and the boy had a lifesaving liver within the week.

Marbin Miller was a mother with a soft spot for children and her stories tore at the heart.

"James 'Jimmy' Alford was the kind of child whom the Department of Children & Families was supposed to protect," she wrote in a story that appeared in the *Herald* in 2002. "But he died, anyway—in a squalid shack on Hard Times Lane in Florida's Panhandle. Jimmy, 14, and his family had been the subject of 23 separate complaints to the state's child-abuse hot line. Over the years, he was beaten with a switch, smacked with a board. He suffered burned fingers, bloody welts. Time and again, investigators from the Department of Children & Families visited his house, examined his injuries and made reports. Still, he died last year, a casualty of questionable casework and poor care. A *Herald* investigation of more than two hundred child deaths statewide has found that flawed probes on the part of the DCF may have contributed to the deaths of at least 100 Florida children over the past five years."

It had been Marbin Miller that Gus Barreiro confided in, in 2006, after viewing a videotape of fourteen-year-old Martin Lee Anderson being punched, kneed, and dragged around a running track by a posse of guards at the Bay County juvenile boot camp. The state had refused the reporter's request to view the incriminating video, so she convinced Barreiro, who chaired the House Juvenile Justice Appropriations Committee at the time, to go on the record with what he saw. In the end, she was able to give a chilling account of what was on the video, in spite of the state's efforts to keep it under wraps.

The story, which ran in the February 9, 2006, edition of the *Herald* began:

> A 14-year-old boy was "brutally" beaten by guards and "flung around like a rag doll" at a boot camp for juvenile delinquents in Panama City hours before he died at a Panhandle hospital, according to two lawmakers who on Wednesday saw a videotape of the incident.
>
> The video, which recorded the last 20 to 30 minutes of the teen's stay at the Bay County Sheriff's Office Boot Camp, shows officers at times kicking, punching and choking Martin Lee Anderson after he refused, or was unable, to comply with officers' orders to run or do other exercises, the legislators said.
>
> Martin, of Panama City, died Jan. 6 at Pensacola's Sacred Heart Hospital, hours after he was admitted to the boot camp, which is operated under a contract with the Florida Department of Juvenile Justice.
>
> The state Department of Law Enforcement, which is investigating Martin's death, showed the camp videotape to two members of the Florida House of Representatives who oversee youth corrections, and at least four members of the governor's staff at FDLE headquarters Wednesday morning.
>
> Clearly shaken, state Rep. Gus Barreiro told the *Miami Herald* that the tape depicted "the most heinous treatment of a human being" he had ever seen. "It was obvious to me

the kid was unconscious, and they were still abusing him. People will be outraged when they see this tape, and they should be outraged."

The case became a cause célèbre and many credited the Miami journalist's painstaking reporting as instrumental in the Florida legislature's vote to close all Florida boot camps, as well as the impetus for the passage of the Martin Lee Anderson Act, the legislation sponsored by Barreiro to revamp the state's juvenile justice system.

The professional relationship between Barreiro and Marbin Miller dated back to 2003, when seventeen-year-old Omar Paisley died in a Miami-Dade juvenile lockup after the staff ignored his cries for medical attention. In a front-page story in the *Herald* that captured national attention, Marbin Miller wrote:

> A supervisor scolded Paisley to "suck it up"—ignore the pain—while a nurse declared, "Ain't nothing wrong with his ass." Paisley, his belly filling with poisons from a ruptured appendix, may have paid for their callousness with his life. Seven boxes of previously unreleased photos, work logs and sworn testimony, part of a Miami-Dade grand jury investigation into the 17-year-old's death, paint a picture of a detention center wracked by chaos the night Paisley died. Paralyzed by fear, trained to eschew independent thought or action, officers took no action until a supervisor finally showed up at Paisley's cell with a wheelchair, handcuffs and shackles. Feeling no pulse, they stopped short of handcuffing a dead child. "Policies and procedures killed Omar Paisley," a Miami-Dade guard testified before lawmakers last week.

Barreiro was at that time beginning his second term as the state representative from Miami, and was chairman of the committee charged with investigating what went wrong in the Paisley case. Profoundly moved by Miller's reporting, he had pushed for drastic change in the policies that had failed Omar Paisley. In the process, Barreiro had become one of Marbin Miller's best sources—the kind she liked most, "off the reservation," meaning he wasn't afraid to take on his own political allies when he smelled injustice—and many of the stories she broke on the juvenile justice beat after that were because of information he fed her.

If anyone could help start the wheels of justice spinning for the victims of the Florida School for Boys, Barreiro told Michael during an early telephone conversation in May, it would be Carol Marbin Miller. As with any successful campaign, Barreiro explained, and Michael knew the lesson well from his experience with the Rosewood case, the public had to buy in, and the best way to recruit support from the public was a front-page story in an influential newspaper.

"You can tell her you're working with me, but no one else can know because, if they find out what I'm doing, I'll lose my job," Barreiro said.

While Barreiro worked quietly behind the scenes at DJJ, trying to find out whatever he could about the reform school—searching old records, talking to people who might know something, and planning his next trip to Marianna—Michael began working on Marbin Miller, trying to convince her that there was a significant story that needed to be told—even if it was fifty years old.

He didn't expect it to be easy.

It was mid-May when Michael dialed the *Miami Herald* and asked for Carol Marbin Miller.

"My name is Michael O'McCarthy and Gus recommended I get in touch with you," Michael said when the reporter answered her phone. "He told me your reporting on the condition of children is the best in the state and that you understand DJJ as well as or better than anyone else around."

Marbin Miller said nothing at first, so Michael continued.

"In 1958–59 I was a prisoner of the Florida School for Boys," he said, rushing to tell as much of the story as he could before she cut him off. "Among other things that happened there, there's a place called the White House where boys were beaten."

Michael quickly recounted his experience at the White House and told Marbin Miller about his coincidental meeting with Robert. There were others coming forward now, he said, albeit in dribs and drabs. The small group of men were calling themselves the White House Boys.

"We're guessing there could be hundreds, maybe thousands of boys who were tortured there," he said. "We don't know how many of them are still alive, but part of our mission is to find them and ask them to come forward with their stories.

"We need strong public support," Michael said, "so we need major news media to cover the story. We want the state of Florida to acknowledge what they did to us."

Marbin Miller listened carefully, assessing the caller and what he said. She wasn't sure what to make of him. Michael was strikingly articulate and convincing, but his story was hard to believe. How could so many boys have been abused and kept quiet for so many years? she wondered. It seemed unlikely that someone wouldn't have come forward long ago. Michael had also talked about his background, and his success in bringing the Rosewood case to light, which she wasn't sure she believed either.

Yet something about his story rang true, so she continued to listen. Perhaps it was the level of detail Michael had that kept Marbin Miller on the phone—despite the fact that a potentially huge story was developing on her beat that day. Detail was always a good measure of a person's credibility. People who lied often spoke in sweeping generalities, and couldn't be pinned down to specifics. Michael had layers of detail and answered each of her questions without pause. Perhaps it was genuineness in his voice. But why come forward after all this time? Marbin Miller wondered aloud.

"Because what happened was wrong," Michael said. "Very wrong. Children were tortured and maybe murdered and no one has ever been held responsible. It's Florida's dirty little secret. We have to come forward, for ourselves, and for the innocent kids who can't come forward."

Marbin Miller was intrigued by Michael's story. She didn't want to rush him off the phone, but she was working on a tip that kids in the state's foster care system, a brother and a sister, had disappeared from their daycare center. Missing foster kids took precedence over everything after little Rilya Wilson disappeared off the face of the earth a few years earlier. Rilya was five years old when she disappeared in 2000, yet it took two years for the state's Department of Children and Families to discover that the little girl was missing from her caretaker's home. All the while, the state caseworker had been filing monthly visit reports that said Rilya was healthy and well. Rilya's caretaker was eventually charged with her murder (and is still awaiting trial) and the DCF chief was forced to resign. It was the biggest story in Florida for months.

Every time a kid went missing, Marbin Miller wondered, "Is this another Rilya?"

"Listen," Marbin Miller told Michael, "I have two missing kids I have to write about, so I really have to go. But let me do some checking and I'll get back to you."

CHAPTER THIRTEEN

Weeks passed and nothing happened. Rosewood had taken three years to get to its rightful conclusion, but Michael couldn't afford to wait that long for resolution in the Marianna case. He was coming unhinged. And he wanted a drink. The urge grew stronger with every day. It had been twenty-three years since he poured his last vodka, still, he could almost taste it now. "Vodka neat," the tingling sensation of the silky liquor touching his tongue, the warmth of the liquid rolling down his throat, the slight burn as it hit his stomach. The second sip was never as delicious as the first, nor was the second drink, or the third. By the third, he wouldn't remember the fourth or the fifth. It didn't matter. The goal was that welcome numbness the excess brought. No more anxiety. No more pain. More than he had in decades, Michael craved that feeling now, thirsted for the soothing poison, as much as he had the first day of his last recovery, when his limbs were spasming from withdrawal and he wailed like a hungry baby for its morning bottle.

When had the yearning begun again? With that introductory

e-mail from Robert? Or was it the moment he realized he was pulling away from his wife Jennifer, because he was beleaguered by old hatred and feared that he couldn't control the rage that seethed within him? Had it been after one of their quarrels over how much she said he'd changed in recent months, or after one of the bad dreams that now invaded his sleep every night?

Had the yearning for that first delicious sip of vodka begun because the bills were piling up, and he hadn't been able to finish the Tubman documentary, not when his mind was racing with thoughts about the White House and Woody and ways he could make things right? Was it that his son and Jennifer's youngest, the same boys who had encouraged them to be together, were now competing for their attention? Or had it started when Robert left to go on the road, depending on him to take over— yet every time Robert checked in for an update he'd had nothing more to report other than that he was working with an anonymous source in Tallahassee (sorry, he couldn't reveal the source's name) and the source was still figuring out how to proceed? And that he also hadn't had much luck convincing a major media source of the story's merit?

Had the yearning for numbness begun because the painful childhood he had buried in his mind had finally emerged and he couldn't muster the strength to fight it?

Or was it that big, blustery Michael O'McCarthy, the intellectual altruist who seemed to have all the answers, redeemer of the weak and the disenfranchised, had again become that bewildered boy who didn't know how to save himself? The same boy who was burdened by the terrible guilt of not being able to save Woody, his reform school friend?

Ultimately, it didn't matter when it began. It wouldn't change the fact that the good life he had worked so hard to build was crumbling before his eyes and he didn't seem to have the power to stop it. He had failed to keep the ghosts of Marianna away, and now he was failing all the other boys who had suffered there—because this David couldn't slay his Goliath unless he could stir up troops.

Was the warrior who led the Rosewood victory too tired to wage this battle? Rosewood had moved at a snail's pace, but he had eagerly soldiered on. Was this battle just too personal? Was it time to surrender?

Take a drink, the voice inside Michael said.

The meeting at the Alano Club on Catalina Drive in Greenville started at noon sharp. Michael pushed through the door to the fellowship room and took a seat on a metal folding chair in the front row, the same spot he had taken week after week, year after year, in his quest to stay sober. People who were serious about their recovery always sat toward the front of the room. Beginners or people who weren't quite sure about their sobriety usually occupied the back rows. Michael fought the urge to join them.

He fidgeted in his seat as he waited for the meeting to begin. Glancing up at the cork ceiling, he noticed the putrid brown stains that had accumulated from years of cigarette smoke—*coffee and cigarettes will keep you sober.* The white poster board with sayings written in black Magic Marker—signs that had been tacked to the wood-paneled walls forever and helped him to "Keep It Simple" and take his sobriety "One Day at a Time" suddenly seemed laughable. What the hell was he doing there anyway? Michael wondered, sitting among these desperate people, some who hung around for most of the day because it was the only way they wouldn't drink. He had been sober long enough to conduct his own meetings, longer than many of the sponsors in the group. But he didn't want to be sober anymore, and all of the self-righteous talk about Jesus and a Higher Power wasn't going to keep him from taking a fucking drink.

An elder spokesman took his seat at the table at the front of the room and called for a moment of silence. Same shit, different day, Michael thought to himself as the man began to pray.

> *God, grant me the serenity*
> *to accept the things I cannot change;*
> *courage to change the things I can;*
> *and wisdom to know the difference.*
> *Amen.*

The crowd echoed "Amen." Michael said nothing.

The leader opened his copy of the Twelve Step book and read a passage: "Lord, make me a channel of thy peace—that where there is hatred, I may bring love—that where there is wrong, I may bring the spirit of forgiveness—that where there is discord, I may bring harmony—that where there is error, I may bring truth—that where there is doubt, I may bring faith—that where there is despair, I may bring hope—that where there are shadows, I may bring light—that where there is sadness, I may bring joy. Lord, grant that I may seek rather to comfort than to be comforted—to understand, than to be understood—to love, than to be loved. For it is by self-forgetting that one finds. It is by forgiving that one is forgiven. It is by dying that one awakens to Eternal Life. Amen."

Michael stared at the man, his pale skin, that long face, the beatific smile. He closed his eyes and saw R. W. Hatton and Troy Tidwell and all of the other "white Christian crackers with Southern drawls" from the reform school that he had learned to loathe. They, too, had quoted scripture and praised the Lord—right before they beat boys into oblivion. That was why Michael didn't believe. How could he? Every time a reference to God came up in his meetings, he replaced it with "It." As a teenager, he had decided that if monsters in Marianna were God's messengers, then he didn't want any part of religion.

Michael was jarred from his thoughts by the spokesman's strident voice.

"Without God there is no recovery," the man bellowed.

Rage gurgled in Michael's throat as he watched the man smile self-righteously at his defenseless disciples.

"Fuck you," Michael muttered, rising from his seat and then walking toward the back of the room and out the door.

Michael closed himself in his home office, first taping a piece of white paper with the words DO NOT DISTURB! on the outside of the door. He needed to get away, so he had come home from the meeting, packed a bag, and arranged a trip to Port Royal in the low country of South Carolina to interview a pair of professors for the Tubman documentary. He could hardly stand being in his own skin. Maybe if he got away from Greenville, from Jennifer, from his encroaching past, he might be able to resist taking that first drink. Maybe.

As he stuffed his briefcase for the next-day trip, Jennifer knocked at the door.

"Michael, what are you doing, where are you going?" she asked.

"Don't knock on the door when I'm working," he shouted, flying into a rage. "Fuck, Jennifer! Why are you interfering with what I'm trying to do? Why don't you understand?"

The door flew open and Jennifer stood there, her face bright red, her body shaking with anger and bewilderment.

"Don't talk to me like that!" she screamed. "What is happening to you, Michael? What are you doing to us? I don't even know you anymore! You promised you were different. I believed you!"

At home, Michael had become emotionally withdrawn and more combative with each passing week. He rarely emerged from his office and when he did he either slept or brooded and he sometimes seemed disoriented. There were moments, when his temper flared, that Jennifer feared him. It was just a feeling, but one she had never thought she would feel about Michael.

Jennifer burst into tears. "Who the hell are you?" she asked, mascara staining her cheeks. "Please, Michael, talk to me!"

Michael grabbed his briefcase and pushed past her. He flew out the front door, the door slamming behind him, and headed to the car. "I'm getting the fuck out of here," he shouted.

Michael had been planning to leave the following morning, drive two hours to Columbia, South Carolina, to meet with the film director of the Tubman project, then head to Port Royal for the interview with the professors. But he couldn't wait. His only thought was getting to Columbia and finding a drink. It was eight o'clock when he checked into the B&B in the heart of the city. An hour later, he was sitting in a bohemian bar called Goatfeathers with the Tubman director. How he loved the merry laughter of the crowd, the pungent smell of the alcohol, the tinkling sound of ice hitting glass. The place reminded him of the hip, hole-in-the-wall kinds of places he once frequented in the Village and in L.A. His mind was made up. No matter the consequences, he was going to drink. He anticipated the first sip, the growing sense of calm, finally, the relief it would bring him.

"What'll y'all have?" the waitress asked.

"A beer," Michael's companion said.

Michael piped up. "And I'll have . . ." Before he could finish his sentence, the waitress, who seemed not to have heard, turned and walked away. The moment of urgency passed and Michael excused himself and walked back to his room to call Jennifer.

"You want to drink, don't you, Michael?" Jennifer asked. How did she know? Michael wondered. How could she possibly know?

"No," he lied. "No, I really don't."

Michael wanted to drink more than anything. More than making things right again with Jennifer. More than finishing his Tubman documentary. More than exposing the evil at Florida School for Boys.

But Michael didn't drink. Not that night.

CHAPTER FOURTEEN

He had his marching orders: Get to the bottom of whatever the trouble is at Marianna and write a report. The best way to do that, Gus Barreiro had convinced his boss, was to embed at the reform school and conduct his own investigation. The top brass at DJJ didn't need to know about his hidden agenda. Not yet.

Barreiro returned to Marianna at the beginning of summer. He got off to a rocky start. His reputation as a maverick was well known and the reform school staff seemed wary of him. On one of his first days on campus, the watch guard in the cafeteria had intervened when Barreiro joined the students in the lunch line. "You're going to eat this crap with these kids?" the guard had asked disbelievingly.

"I am," Barreiro replied, undeterred.

The disconnect that Barreiro sensed between the workers and the students at the institution was troublesome. He had seen it so many times before, this sort of institutional antipathy toward problem children. In his many years of dealing with juvenile delinquents, Barreiro had learned that all too often the people who worked in the system were in it for the wrong reasons. You could teach people the mechanics of running a program, but you couldn't teach heart or compassion, and Barreiro didn't see much of either at Marianna.

Over the years, Barreiro had encountered dozens of men and women who worked with troubled kids, who seemed to take pride in beating them down. "Kids change for people, not for barbed wire," he would preach when the opportunity arose. "At the end of the day, this is still someone's child." Dissenters would shake their heads, as if to say he was just another clueless bleeding heart who didn't know what the hell he was talking about. Barreiro knew what they were thinking: *You don't have to make a living dealing with these punks. Our job is to teach these little bastards a lesson.*

The staff at Marianna was typical of such an attitude, Barreiro thought. For the most part, they were uneducated and insufficiently trained. Many were qualified to pump gas or bag groceries, but they had no credentials in juvenile reform and they didn't particularly like their work. But state jobs paid more than the local gas station or grocery store and the benefits were good. If you were looking to feed a family, the reform school was the only game in town. It had been so for decades.

Perhaps even more tragic than Marianna was that the blueprint for the school was the same one that had been used for correctional institutions across the country. Reform schools and prisons were typically placed in remote areas where jobs were scarce and the hiring pool was inexperienced and unskilled. The workers came from the same socioeconomic backgrounds as the inmates. Most were overworked and underpaid. They had few resources to help the students and even less oversight in their treatment of them. Rather than any altruistic desire to help the unfortunate boys, their custodians were more often than not in it just for the paycheck. But it didn't take long to realize the paycheck hardly covered the cost of the frustration they felt. The guards tended to dehumanize the inmates, which opened the door for the brutality. They got away with their transgressions because they were out in the middle of nowhere, and their colleagues either weren't watching or chose to look the other way. As far as Barreiro could tell, not much had changed over the years.

In 2008, the staff at Marianna was still treating their inmates as prisoners, not disturbed children, and Barreiro believed that was exactly the wrong approach. Many of the guards saw the whole of their jobs as keeping the young offenders under control—no matter what it took. Why did they treat children so harshly? Because they could, Barreiro would say.

The way Barreiro saw it, the bottom of an organization reflected the top, and the people at the apex of the state's juvenile justice system were focused more on their own careers than they were on the children they were charged with fostering. The people who worked in the trenches, on the other hand, were suffering from a toxic mix of frustration and isolation, which they often took out on the children.

Barreiro got a firsthand look at the drill one afternoon when he was working in an office on campus and happened to glance out the window just as a guard violently shoved a boy to the ground. The crying boy, who Barreiro knew as Jimmy, came running into the office, frantically trying to get away. Judging from the rapid pounding of boots on the hallway floor, the guard was in furious pursuit. "Stay here with me," Barreiro had told the terrified boy. The guard stopped short when he saw Barreiro. His adrenaline was pumping so hard that his face was purple and his eyes bulged out of his head.

"Calm down, man," Barreiro said, standing toe to toe with the guard. "Take a deep breath." Barreiro sent Jimmy back to his dorm, and sat with the guard until he composed himself. A week later, he ran into Jimmy. The boy had a black eye. "What happened?" Barreiro asked. "Oh, I fell and hit my face on the sink," Jimmy replied. Barreiro didn't buy it. He believed the boy had lied in order to survive.

There had been plenty of work to do in Marianna. Boys told Barreiro that guards randomly beat them and that when they weren't being punished they were treated with indifference by the staff. Many said they felt hopeless and depressed. Barreiro's goal was to turn the institution from a prison into a program to help juvenile offenders become law-abiding men. He suggested small changes: that the boys be allowed to shower in the morning; that the food be improved; that they not have to wear stripes. "Let's train people how to relate to these kids," Barreiro had said during a staff meeting one day. From the looks on their faces, he wasn't sure they understood.

For the forty-five days he spent at the reform school, Barreiro had Michael in the back of his mind. He had come to Marianna, determined to pursue what he had started on his first visit there. Whenever he had the opportunity, he asked people at the school and in town what they knew about the history of the institution. Did they know about this place called the White House, where boys had been beaten and tortured? Had they heard about beatings that had gotten out of control? Just as had happened on his inaugural trip, everyone he questioned said, yes, they had heard things. Even the young waitress at the local Ruby Tuesday's had a story. Her grandmother, she said, worked in the cafeteria at the reform school and "she told us they killed boys there."

The more Barreiro heard, the more determined he was to do right by O'McCarthy and the other men who had suffered at the hands of the state of Florida. The desperation in O'McCarthy's voice had resonated with Barreiro. It was the same voice of so many of the abused children he had listened to over the years. A pleading voice, laced with wariness and sadness—profound sadness. Because they had been robbed of the most basic tenet of childhood: protection.

"Everyone knew," Barreiro said to an old-timer at the school one day. "Everyone knew that kids were being tortured here, yet no one ever did anything about it."

The man shrugged.

How could an entire community be so indifferent? Barreiro wondered. So callous? He couldn't get his head around it.

But his most shocking discovery was still to come.

It was at the tail end of his stay in Marianna. Barreiro was having lunch with a group of local officials at the Jackson County Corrections Institution next door to the School for Boys. The prison property had once been the North Side, "the colored side," of the reform school before it was desegregated in 1968. Barreiro raised the subject of the school and its storied past. Someone in the group mentioned an old cemetery on the premises.

"Where is it?" Barreiro asked.

"I can take you there," Ted Jeter, the prison warden said.

The trip took just a few minutes by car. Jeter drove about six hundred yards on a rugged trail through the woods behind the prison when they came upon a clearing. There stood rows of rusty white crosses. Barreiro counted thirty-one. A chill ran through him. The crosses were cracked and weathered, but the grass was freshly cut. They had no names. Who was buried beneath those crosses? Barreiro wondered aloud. And who was tending the old graveyard? Jeter said he didn't know.

Barreiro thought about the stories he'd been told about boys disappearing from the school and never being seen again. He thought about the stories of boys being beaten to death. My God, he thought. Are these their graves?

He reached into his pocket and pulled out his cell phone to photograph the crosses, then returned to the reform school to inquire about the cemetery. Superintendent Mary Zahasky, who was relatively new on the job, pleaded ignorance. She didn't even know there was a cemetery, she said. But Milton Mooneyham, who had worked there for decades, said the school maintained it. Had for as long as he could remember, Mooneyham said.

"So who's buried there?" Barreiro asked.

"I reckon I don't know."

"So you've been maintaining this cemetery, but no one has ever questioned who's buried there?" Barreiro asked.

"You should let the dead lie dead," Zahasky interjected. "You don't want to open up a can of worms."

Barreiro felt dizzy from the thoughts swirling in his head. Are kids really buried there? he wondered. And if so, had their parents even been notified of their deaths? It was inconceivable to think all thirty-one had been orphans. If their families had been informed of their deaths, why would the children be buried there? Wouldn't the families have brought their children's remains home to be buried? Had some received those telegrams saying "Dear Sir and Ma'am. We regret to inform you that your son has run away from the school," then been kept wondering what had become of their child for the rest of their lives? Had their letters gone unanswered? Had mothers and fathers died with the anguish of not knowing what had become of their sons?

What was he supposed to do? Barreiro wondered. Make a report to DJJ and nothing would come of it? Michael O'McCarthy's incredible tale of systematic torture and perhaps even murder had suddenly gained credibility, he thought.

Barreiro returned to the graveyard the following day. The sun peaked through the fluttering trees, casting streaks of brilliant light on the rows of shabby crosses. He shook off a chill. For a while he just stood there, staring at the anonymous markers, imagining the abject sorrow of the parents who had lost their little boys. Thinking about how defenseless O'McCarthy and all the other boys had been, so far from home, isolated and at the mercy of a few cruel men.

A few minutes passed. Barreiro took the cell phone from his pocket and punched in the number for the *Miami Herald*. It was Gandhi who had said, "Injustice must be made visible."

"Carol," Barreiro said when Marbin Miller answered the call, "I'm in Marianna. I'm standing on a kid's grave. I'm sending you the pictures."

Next, he called Michael.

"I'm sorry, Michael," he said, "I know it's been a while. But I haven't forgotten you. I'm in Marianna now. I've been talking to people here for weeks. Did you know about these graves?"

"No," Michael said. "There were always rumors about boys dying, but I never heard anything about unmarked graves."

"Michael," Barreiro said, "I don't know how long it will take, but I will do anything I have to do to get you boys justice. That is my promise to you."

"But what about protecting yourself? Your job?" Michael asked, knowing Barreiro was facing adversity from his colleagues at the DJJ.

"I don't care about myself," Barreiro said. "We have to move forward on this, no matter where it takes us. I believe the truth will win out."

CHAPTER FIFTEEN

"If only there were evil people somewhere insidiously committing evil deeds and it were necessary only to separate them from the rest of us and destroy them. But the line dividing good and evil cuts through the heart of every human being."
—Soviet dissident and Nobel laureate Aleksandr Solzhenitsyn

The man seated quietly in a pew at the First Baptist Church in Marianna doesn't look capable of monstrous acts. He looks rather ordinary. His skin is the kind of translucent pale that comes in the dusk of life, and his colorless hair is combed neatly back. A pair of old-fashioned wire-rimmed glasses hovers on the bridge of his nose, and a pristine dark suit jacket over an open-collar shirt gives him an air of propriety.

If you look closely you can see that one of his jacket sleeves is empty.

His family would tell you that the eighty-four-year-old parishioner who is waiting for the Sunday-morning service to begin is a simple man who lives for his children and grandchildren. A man who is capable of great emotion, who worked hard all his life to support his family. Before he retired in 1982, even after a hard day on the job, he would jump in to help his wife wash the dinner dishes when she was too tired to finish. In his heyday, the man loved to foxtrot and, boy, he could cut a rug. He was known to have a little bit of the flirt in him. And he was sentimental. He cried like a baby when his grown granddaughter Tiffany sang to him, and when his little dog Scotty died he was sad for weeks afterward.

Like everyone, the man had his foibles. People who worked for him remember his obsession for perfection; if his finger came up dusty when he ran it over a doorsill there would be hell to pay. And his second wife left him after only two years of marriage because she felt suffocated by his possessiveness and his tight control.

What everyone agrees on is that the man has always been a dapper dresser. He wore suit jackets even when the occasion didn't call for such formality, but not so much as a custom as to hide his missing left arm. When he was six years old, he leaned on the barrel of his daddy's loaded shotgun and accidentally shot it off. Almost eighty years later, he was still so self-conscious about it that when he went to a restaurant he sat with his left side to the wall.

Troy Tidwell hated it when people called him "the one-armed man."

The Stanford Prison Experiment is the gold standard of studies on the ability of ordinary people to do evil things. Nearly four decades old, it is still the body of research that professionals point to when they talk about the complicated psychology of evil, and whether it is an inherent trait in some, or a chosen behavior of which many seemingly average people are capable.

The landmark 1971 study began with a classified ad that said simply: "Male college students needed for psychological study of prison life. $15 per day for 1–2 weeks beginning Aug. 14. For further information and applications, come to Room 248, Jordan Hall, Stanford U." A team of researchers led by Stanford University psychology professor Philip Zimbardo selected twenty-four college-aged males from the seventy who responded. Those who were chosen had tested as the most psychologically sound of the applicants, the most "normal." The roles of the inmates and guards were determined with a coin toss. Zimbardo played the prison superintendent and his research assistant, David Jaffe, the warden.

The experiment commenced on the Sunday morning of August 17, 1971 (coincidentally, three days before Michael O'McCarthy's comrade George Jackson was shot and killed by guards at San Quentin) with a surprise roundup of the "prisoners" at their homes by the Palo Alto police. The prisoners were charged with armed robbery and burglary and booked at the county jail. There, they were read their Miranda rights and their mug shots and fingerprints were taken. Blindfolded, they were then driven to a simulated lockup in the basement of Stanford University's psychology department where they were assigned numbers, stripped naked and searched, and given smocks and stocking caps to wear.

The "guards" who awaited them at the mock prison were all dressed identically in official-looking khaki uniforms and they wore mirrored sunglasses to inhibit any eye contact with the prisoners. Researchers had provided them with whistles and billy clubs and instructions to maintain control of the prison, in whatever way they saw fit, except for inflicting physical harm on the inmates. At orientation the day before, Zimbardo told the guards: "You can create in the prisoners feelings of boredom, a sense of fear to some degree, you can create a notion of arbitrariness that their life is totally controlled by us, by the system, you, me, and they'll have no privacy. . . . We're going to take away their individuality in various ways. In general what all this leads to is a sense of powerlessness. That is, in this situation we'll have all the power and they'll have none."

The experiment, which was supposed to last two weeks, went quickly awry. On the second day, the prisoners became fed up with being objectified and they staged a rebellion, "taunting and cursing the guards." The guards attacked back with fire extinguishers. In further retaliation, "they broke into each cell, stripped the prisoners naked, took the beds out, forced the ringleaders of the prisoner rebellion into solitary confinement, and generally began to harass and intimidate the prisoners," Zimbardo and his team later wrote in a summary of the experiment.

The rebellion had fashioned "greater solidarity among the guards," the researchers observed. "Now, suddenly, it was no longer just an experiment, no longer a simple simulation. Instead, the guards saw the prisoners as troublemakers who were out to get them, who might really cause them some harm. In response to this threat, the guards began stepping up their control, surveillance, and aggression."

The guards fell into three categories, the researchers found: The "tough but fair guards who followed prison rules." The "good guy" guards, "who did little favors for the prisoners and never punished them." And the others, who were "hostile, arbitrary, and inventive in their forms of prisoner humiliation. These guards appeared to thoroughly enjoy the power they wielded, yet none of our preliminary personality tests were able to predict this behavior," the researchers wrote.

As the pressure inside the prison mounted, the guards became more aggressive. They ratcheted up punishments to include a protracted exercise regimen, a tactic that had been used in Nazi concentration camps, and ordered the inmates to do demeaning chores, for instance, cleaning out toilet bowls with their bare hands. They refused the prisoners bathroom privileges and took away their mattresses, forcing them to sleep on concrete. The prisoners were subjected to sexual humiliation at one point, made to strip naked and simulate sodomy on each other. Some were locked in solitary confinement in a tiny, dark closet the guards called "the hole."

The prisoners quickly cracked under the stress: After the first thirty-six hours, "Prisoner #8612 began suffering from acute emotional disturbance, disorganized thinking, uncontrollable crying, and rage," the researchers noted in their findings. "#8612 then began to act 'crazy,' to scream, to curse, to go into a rage that seemed out of control. It took quite a while before we became convinced that he was really suffering and that we had to release him."

The more vulnerable the prisoners became, the more sadistically the guards behaved. Some of the worst abuses took place in the middle of the night, when the guards thought no one was observing their behavior. "They steadily increased their coercive aggression tactics, humiliation and dehumanization of the prisoners," Zimbardo told the *Stanford News* in 1997. "The staff had to frequently remind the guards to refrain from such tactics." Still, he said, the deteriorating conditions "resulted in extreme stress reactions that forced us to release five prisoners, one a day, prematurely."

After six days, the experiment had to be called off.

———

"When we planned our two-week-long simulation of prison life, we sought to understand more about the process by which people called 'prisoners' lose their liberty, civil rights, independence and privacy, while those called 'guards' gain social power by accepting the responsibility for controlling and managing the lives of their dependent charges," Zimbardo wrote in an article entitled "A Pirandellan Prison" in the April 8, 1973, *New York Times Magazine*.

In the process of studying the relationship between the prisoners and the guards Zimbardo and his research team discovered what they considered to be solid anecdotal proof that even moral people were capable of committing malevolent acts, given the right circumstances, and that power, not people, precipitated evil.

The Stanford experiment bolstered the then-controversial conclusions of a 1961 experiment by Yale professor and social psychologist Stanley Milgram, whose focus was the willingness of ordinary people to obey the will of authority figures, even when it conflicted with their own moral conscience. Milgram outlined the nuts and bolts of his experiment in the 1974 book *Obedience to Authority:* "Two people come to a psychology laboratory to take part in a study of memory and learning," he wrote. "One of them is designated as a 'teacher' and the other a 'learner.' The experimenter explains that the study is concerned with the effects of punishment on learning. The learner is conducted into a room, seated in a chair, his arms strapped down to prevent excessive movement, and an electrode attached to his wrist. He is told that he is to learn a list of word pairs; whenever he makes an error, he will receive electric shocks of increasing intensity."

The real focus of the experiment is the teacher, Milgram explained. After watching the learner being strapped in the chair, the teacher is taken to a separate room and seated at a control panel, called a "shock generator," with thirty switches of accelerating voltage. The teacher is instructed to ask the learner a series of questions. For each wrong answer, he is told to administer shocks that are progressively more painful. What the teacher doesn't know is that the learner is an actor, and there is no shock. "The results of the experiment are both surprising and dismaying," Milgram wrote.

"Before the experiments, I sought predictions about the outcome from various kinds of people—psychiatrists, college sophomores, middle-class adults, graduate students and faculty in the behavioral sciences," Milgram wrote in a 1974 article in *Harper's* magazine, entitled "The Perils of Obedience." "With remarkable similarity, they predicted that virtually all the subjects would refuse to obey the experimenter. The psychiatrist, specifically, predicted that most subjects would not go beyond 150 volts, when the victim makes his first explicit demand to be freed . . . and that only a pathological fringe . . . would administer the highest shock on the board. These predictions were unequivocally wrong."

Of the forty teachers in Milgram's first experiment, twenty-five obeyed the orders of the experimenter to the bitter end, sometimes punishing the learner until he begged to be released from the study. Milgram concluded that when "stark authority was pitted against the subjects' strongest moral imperatives against hurting others, and, with the subjects' ears ringing with the screams of the victims, authority won more often than not. The extreme willingness of adults to go to almost any lengths on the command of an authority constitutes the chief finding of the study and the fact most urgently demanding explanation."

So much for the idea that only the rare genetic sadist is capable of such extreme cruelty to his fellow man, Milgram concluded.

"The condition of the experiment undermines another commonly offered explanation of the subjects' behavior—that those who shocked the victim at the most severe levels came only from the sadistic fringe of society," he wrote in the *Harper's* article. "If one considers that almost two-thirds of the participants fall into the category of 'obedient' subjects, and that they represented ordinary people drawn from working, managerial, and professional classes, the argument becomes very shaky."

Milgram juxtaposed his findings with a highly controversial premise posed by Hannah Arendt in her book about Nazi Adolf Eichmann, the so-called architect of the Holocaust: that Eichmann was not so much evil incarnate as a good soldier in an immoral conflict.

"Indeed, it is highly reminiscent of the issue that arose in connection with Hannah Arendt's 1963 book, *Eichmann in Jerusalem*," Milgram wrote. "Arendt contended that the prosecution's effort to depict Eichmann as a sadistic monster was fundamentally wrong, that he came closer to being an uninspired bureaucrat who simply sat at his desk and did his job. For asserting her views, Arendt became the object of considerable scorn, even calumny. Somehow it was felt that the monstrous deeds carried out by Eichmann required a brutal, twisted personality, evil incarnate. After witnessing hundreds of ordinary persons submit to the authority in our own experiments, I must conclude that Arendt's conception of the banality of evil comes closer to the truth than one might dare imagine."

In his book *Evil—Inside Human Violence and Cruelty*, Roy F. Baumeister offers up the Polish sociologist Zygmund Bauman's contention that the Holocaust was directed by a "gardener's mentality," and is more prevalent in society than one would like to believe. "A gardener is raising flowers and other plants in accordance with a particular plan for a beautiful, fine place," Baumeister wrote. "The weeds must be removed to make this vision reality. Some gardeners may hate the weeds, while others may regard them merely as an inconvenience. In the end, however, it doesn't matter much what the gardeners' feelings are: Both types of gardeners end up killing the weeds."

Was it possible that Troy Tidwell and his Marianna cohorts were simply uninspired bureaucrats doing what was expected of them? Were they good soldiers carrying out the tenets of a debauched system sanctioned by the state?

Even today, if you talk to people in Marianna about the Florida School for Boys and its long history of brutality, they'll tell you that the family members and neighbors who worked with "those boys" were good men who were just doing their jobs, and that sometimes it took extreme measures to maintain order.

In other words, they were just trying to control the weeds.

CHAPTER SIXTEEN

Gus Barreiro had a dilemma. He had learned plenty since his first conversation with Michael O'McCarthy several months earlier. Boys—hundreds, perhaps thousands of boys—had been tortured and some possibly even punished to death at Marianna. How many lives had been ruined because of the actions of a few sadistic government employees with too much power? he wondered. How many crimes had been committed on state time? What Barreiro knew, what he believed, was that the state had an obligation to acknowledge its own culpability in what had the potential to be the worst case of institutional child abuse in Florida's history. He also knew that getting justice for the victims would be tricky.

Barreiro had watched juvenile justice in action for years. He considered himself an expert in how the agency operated. When a problem arose that put DJJ in a bad light, the inclination was to deny, deny, deny. If denial failed, the follow-up strategy was to circle the wagons and stall, hoping that eventually the media and the public would lose interest. In Barreiro's experience, the agency had never been forthcoming about anything in which even the slightest controversy was involved. The general philosophy seemed to be to avoid taking responsibility for anything that went wrong in the system, at all costs.

If the department hadn't been willing to come clean on Omar Paisley or Martin Lee Anderson, where the evidence against state employees was obvious, and in Anderson's case even caught on camera, then getting it to admit a fifty-year-old catastrophe based on the fading memories of a few older men was a long shot at best. Before Barreiro could even think about approaching his superiors with the charges being made, he had to know what the victims were looking for.

In late summer, Barreiro contacted Michael to ask the question.

"What do you guys want?" Barreiro asked.

"We want the state of Florida to acknowledge what it did to us," Michael said. "We want to be able to go on the grounds of the school, see the White House again, anything we need to do to try to get some closure."

It was a long shot to expect the state to acknowledge such abject negligence, especially when doing so would invite damning publicity and compensation for the victims. But Michael was adamant that the group accept nothing less. Such an admission by the state would go a long way to helping him and the other White House Boys feel relevant and whole, and to bolstering their credibility with a public that was bound to be skeptical about fifty-year-old memories. He also wanted assurance that, should any of the perpetrators still be living, they be held accountable for their acts. For Michael, anything short of full acknowledgment by the state would mean that he had failed himself and his reform school brothers.

"How many of you are there now?" Barreiro asked.

"Right now there are six of us," O'McCarthy said. "We expect that there could be dozens and maybe hundreds at some point. We're not going away."

"I'll get back to you," Barreiro said.

Barreiro had chosen his strategy carefully. The worst thing he could do was alarm the bosses at DJJ. The agency was well known for its defensive posture and even a hint of scandal would send the top brass into shutdown mode. The plan was that he would begin by soft-pedaling the story. His first pitch would be to Frank Penela, DJJ's communications director. It was Penela's job to divert controversy away from the agency. If Barreiro could get him to bite, there was a chance the plan could work.

Barreiro began the conversation with Penela dispassionately. There was this guy, he said, a Michael O'McCarthy, from South Carolina, who had approached him recently with shocking claims about the Florida School for Boys. At first, Barreiro said, he had dismissed O'McCarthy's tale of torture and tragedy as the exaggerated memories of one troubled man. But he had done some poking around, and what he had discovered seemed to back what O'McCarthy was saying. There were other men, all strangers to each other, who had the same excruciating memories of Marianna, Barreiro said, and they had recently banded together to form a small group, calling themselves the White House Boys. O'McCarthy was the spokesman and he was a savvy activist with plenty of know-how about exposing social injustices, Barreiro said. There was more, though, he said cautiously. Nearly everyone he had spoken with when he was in Marianna a few weeks earlier seemed to know that terrible things went on at the reform school. Many claimed to have knowledge about brutal beatings and boys being killed in years past. It was an open secret in the little, out-of-the-way town. The best way to keep it contained there, Barreiro suggested, was for the agency to work with the men who were making the accusations. Work with them or risk losing control of the story, he said.

"This thing has the potential to blow wide open," Barreiro told Penela. "We really should get out in front of it."

Penela sat back in his chair, wringing his hands and staring straight ahead. He looked concerned, Barreiro thought.

It wouldn't take much to make this go away, Barreiro went on, gently pushing his agenda. The men were only looking for closure. They wanted to be allowed to stand on reform school soil to confront their pasts. They wanted to be able to walk inside the White House. They wanted the state to acknowledge that it had failed the children at the Florida School for Boys. What would be the harm of that?

"Let's embrace this thing," Barreiro said. "If we don't, it's going to look like we're covering up. We'll end up with a bunch of men holding a candlelight vigil outside the school gates and media swarming all over it.

"If we handle it right, Frank, we could look like heroes," Barreiro added, pressing his case.

The air crackled with a tense silence. Neither man said anything for a few minutes. Penela seemed to be weighing the options, and Barreiro struggled to keep his composure. Had he succeeded in convincing Penela that owning up to the failure was the best course of action? he wondered. Would Penela buy into his idea to allow the men on the Marianna campus? Or would he politely dismiss him? Dismiss them? Barreiro sat quietly. *C'mon,* he thought to himself. *Do the right thing, Frank. Do the right thing, damn it!*

Penela finally spoke. Yes, he said, the situation had the potential to become a public relations nightmare. Something had to be done. The state couldn't simply ignore the men and risk the media getting wind of it. Penela promised to continue the discussion with Bonnie Rogers, the agency's chief of staff, and Rod Love, it's deputy director. He would seek direction from them as to how to proceed.

"I'll wait to hear from you then," Barreiro said, trying to conceal his elation.

Barreiro fought the urge to jump out of his chair. *I didn't get a "no,"* he thought as he strode out of the executive suite to return to his own office, two floors below. *I didn't get a "no"!* he sang to himself after the elevator doors closed. *I didn't get a "no"!*

Now all Barreiro needed was a date. If Rogers and Love agreed to allow the White House Boys to visit the reform school, and a date was formally placed on the government calendar, it would be difficult for the department to back out. That had been Barreiro's plan: to push his agenda to the point of no return.

Now all he could do was cross his fingers and wait.

CHAPTER SEVENTEEN

The roiling surf sparkled aquamarine beneath the vivid Caribbean sun and, off in the distance, commercial fishing boats bobbed in the bay. Jennifer giggled as she looked across the table at Michael. It had been months since things had seemed so easy between them. Puerto Viejo in August was normally soggy, but on this evening the air was light and the sky was a clear blue slate. A new friend from town had recommended the eclectic restaurant on the famous Salsa Brava surfing beach in the seaside town. Michael and Jennifer had taken a taxi there from their little seaside cottage. Sitting there, under a thatched roof, the peal of reggae music fusing with the sound of the crashing surf, Jennifer thought that maybe she and Michael really could put the nightmare of the White House behind them in this beautiful place. She took another sip of her cocktail and proposed a toast.

"To our future here," she said, clinking her fresh mint mojito with Michael's glass of tepid sparkling water.

"To our future," Michael said, raising his glass and grinning for the first time in weeks.

The move to Costa Rica had been in the works for months and right until the plane took off from Miami International Airport, Jennifer thought it was possible that she and her twelve-year-old son Billy would end up living alone in paradise. It had been Michael's dream to call the peaceful Central American country home. He had vacationed there for ten years and fallen in love with the Costa Rican ethos. There was no place like it in the world, Michael had told Jennifer when they first met. There was a reason it was named "The Rich Coast," he said. Imagine living in a land with free health care, no army, and such a fierce commitment to the well-being of the environment that it had been named the greenest country in the world. Perhaps she would consider taking the adventure with him?

At first, Jennifer thought he was crazy. They barely knew each other and he was proposing that they move together to another country. Even after they married and started the discussion about moving, Jennifer had been hesitant about leaving the South—it was all she had ever known—but after a while she began to see things Michael's way. For her whole life, she had wanted to live on the ocean, breathe the salt air, and be lulled to sleep by the sound of the waves, and the idea of living in the Caribbean was exciting. The move could be a great adventure, she thought, and they could always come back to the States if their tropical fantasy didn't last. As the time to leave drew near, though, and Michael continued to spiral into his miserable past, Jennifer began to doubt her decision.

Things came to a head on that day, a week earlier, in the Miami airport. Michael had fallen into one of his worst funks yet as they waited to board the flight to San José. His mood that afternoon swung from pouting and verging on tears to hissing at

Jennifer that she didn't understand what he was going through, it was the worst possible time to be leaving the States in light of his work with Robert. He felt as if he was abandoning his White House brothers; how could he continue his work from so far away? Jennifer tried to understand, to empathize with her distraught husband, but it was too late to turn back, she explained gently. They had given up their home in Greenville, paid to have all of their belongings put in storage, left her older son and Michael's boy behind and taken Billy out of school and prepared him for the dramatic lifestyle change. A new life awaited in Costa Rica, Jennifer said, trying to sound upbeat. Remember how excited they had been to get there? Where would they go if they didn't board the plane then? she asked, almost pleadingly. He could stay in contact with Robert by phone, and travel back to the States when he was needed. Michael had become increasingly hostile with each of Jennifer's questions. He didn't have any answers, he cried. He just wanted to be left alone, goddamn it. Finally losing her patience, Jennifer had taken Billy by the hand and moved away from Michael, storming past the other passengers waiting at the gate. At that point she didn't care if he boarded the plane or not. But he had, and his mood had been darkening ever since.

Yet here they were, alone for the first time in how long, sharing a romantic dinner on a Costa Rican beach and happily twittering about this and that. Jennifer didn't want the perfect evening to end. It had been months since Michael seemed so carefree; weeks since she had seen his blue eyes sparkle or heard the tinkle of his funny giggle. The brief respite from reality seemed to be just what they needed, Jennifer thought, as the waves rolled onto the crystalline sand and the aroma of Creole cooking wafted in the air. If only they could stay in the moment, she thought. If only they could stay there, in that funky little beach hut, with the friendly people and the happy music. Maybe everything would be all right after all. Maybe the worst was finally over, and they would go home to Billy and their little house by the water and live happily ever after.

For the first time in months, things felt the way they once did with Michael. It had been so long since they'd had fun together. So long since they'd shared silly banter ("Uh oh. It's seven thirty. It's past our curfew. We'd better call Billy for permission to stay out later."). It had been so long since they had been the Michael and Jennifer they were before the Florida School for Boys barged into their idyllic life together.

They splurged on dinner that night. Calamari, ceviche, arroz con mariscos, carne guisada. The mojitos were sweet and delicious. A tiny bit giddy, Jennifer ordered a second, then another. Michael had always said that someone else's social drinking didn't bother him. He'd been sober for too long to be tempted, he said. Drink up, Jennifer, he said. Have one for me.

"Let's go dancing," Jennifer said, feeling tipsy after draining her third drink. "C'mon, Michael. We've never gone dancing together. We're free! Let's party a little!"

"What should I drink if we go out dancing?" Michael asked, a question that seemed peculiar to Jennifer.

"I don't know," she stuttered. "I guess, Pellegrino?"

They laughed an uneasy laugh and Jennifer began talking about something trivial, when Michael interrupted: "If I was going to drink, what should I drink?" he asked, persisting. The festive mood began to fade as Jennifer focused on her husband's eyes, trying to gauge whether he was serious or not. She feared he was, but she wasn't prepared to believe it.

"I don't know what you like," she replied, trying to shake a growing sense of foreboding.

"What if I ever decided to drink?" Michael asked.

Jennifer felt as if the merry-go-round she had been riding had suddenly grinded to a halt and she could either grab on or be thrown off. She told Michael that she understood how difficult it must be to stay sober, how the temptation to drink must surely be great, even after all these years, and how proud she was that he had been sober for so long. Perhaps it hadn't been such a good idea to come into this lively town at night, she said, where everywhere you looked you saw people flowing out of discos and sidewalk cafes with drinks in their hands. She shouldn't have had so many mojitos and lost her head, she said. She was sorry she had overindulged. It was inconsiderate of her, but she had thought, he had always told her, he didn't mind when someone drank in his presence. She really didn't want dessert, and she didn't want to go to a disco, after all, Jennifer said. She was happy just to go back home and watch a movie.

Jennifer was terrified. She could feel Michael wavering on his long sobriety and she wasn't sure she could stop him from taking a drink. Why had she never thought she would be in such a position? Not with Michael, the man who had offered her tea or Coca-Cola every time she visited during those early days of their dating. He had been sober too long to relapse. She had never given the idea of him drinking again a second thought. But after he had become involved in the reform school campaign, he had stopped attending his meetings, and lately he had been talking a lot about being the keeper of his own sobriety—taking charge of his own recovery, he had called it. He didn't need anyone else to help him stay sober, he said.

So why was she so surprised that he was thinking about a drink? Jennifer didn't know what to do.

"Michael," she said, trying to sound supportive, "I know you're in a great deal of pain and I want to help you through it, the way you helped me when I needed you. But if you ever decide to drink again, please make sure I'm with you."

If he was going to drink, she wanted to at least be there to take care of him, to protect him from himself, she told herself. But Michael took what she said as a provocation. Go ahead. I dare you.

"Okay, I'm going to do it," Michael said, taking the perceived challenge.

"Please don't," Jennifer said, forgetting about the moon and the surf, the coral reefs and the glittering sand.

"Will you have another?" he asked, pointing to her empty glass.

Jennifer said nothing. Summoning the waitress, Michael ordered another mojito for her and an Irish coffee for himself. Irish whiskey was Hemingway's drink, he said, merrily. A class act, that guy. A helluva writer, too. And boy could he pound 'em back!

Jennifer didn't speak at first. Then she quietly asked Michael to cancel the drink order. No, he said, he could see the bar from his seat. It was too late. The Irish coffee was already made. Shouldn't waste! Michael smiled when the tray of drinks arrived. The waitress set the mojito in front of Jennifer, then the spiked coffee by

Michael. Jennifer sat there, paralyzed, watching him blow the steam away from his hot alcoholic drink. She grabbed the cup and sipped it.

"You won't like it," she said. "Ick. It's terrible. I wouldn't waste my time if I were you." Fighting off the urge to be sick, she added, "C'mon, Michael. Let's just go home."

Michael wouldn't hear it. "I thought we were going dancing?" he asked. Jennifer thought he sounded as if he were taunting her.

"Please, Michael," she pleaded. "Let's go. You don't want the drink."

"You're the one who challenged me," Michael said.

Jennifer was incredulous. Challenged him? Challenged him? She had been trying to be supportive when she offered to be there if he did decide to drink. She certainly didn't want him to drink. She knew all too well how that would end.

Michael slowly raised the cup to his lips.

"You don't have to do this. Please," Jennifer pleaded. "There's no reason for you to drink that."

Michael said nothing, but tipped the cup and drank. With a single sip, he had wiped out twenty-three years of hard-fought sobriety. He swirled the liquor around his mouth. The taste of the pungent alcohol combined with the sugary coffee was horrible. It reminded him of those last days of his drinking career, when he had reached the point of retching every time alcohol passed his lips. Rather than stop drinking, he had switched to a toxic concoction of Jack Daniel's and peppermint schnapps, appropriately named a Snakebite. The schnapps had made the hard liquor go down easier, but the taste had disgusted him. Or maybe what had disgusted him back then was the fact that he needed a fix so desperately he would have chugged rubbing alcohol if he could have swallowed it.

"Oh my God," Jennifer said disbelievingly. "You really did it. You really took a drink, didn't you?"

Michael smiled and replaced the cup on the table. "Of course not, silly," he lied. He had just swirled the warm liquid around in his mouth then spit it back in the cup without swallowing.

"It was terrible," he said. "Awful. I didn't even want it. Now let's call a taxi and go home."

"Okay," Jennifer said, wanting desperately to believe her husband.

But Michael knew it wasn't his last sip. He knew he was going to drink. Not tonight, but he would drink. Something had to ease his swelling pain.

CHAPTER EIGHTEEN

Carol Marbin Miller had been quietly going about educating herself about the Florida School for Boys. Her early digging turned up the reform school's long and infamous past: the children chained in leg irons; the boys who had been trapped in their burning dormitory while the guards were up to no good in town; the dark, cold isolation cells; the 1980s lawsuit to stop the continued chaining and hogtying of the students. The troublesome history had given Michael O'McCarthy's story new and crucial credibility. Good reporters had a sense for people and an ear for the truth. After many conversations with Michael, Marbin Miller had come to believe that he was genuine and that his memories of abuse were real. The stories of a handful of other men that Michael had steered her way also rang true.

These men had been able to repeat sights, sounds, and smells from fifty years ago. Although they had been at the school at different times, their memories were strikingly similar and there was nothing to suggest they had collaborated on their accounts. On the contrary, Michael, Robert, and the others with whom they had joined forces seemed genuinely astounded by the parallels of their experiences. Each had independently spoken of specks of flesh on the mattress where they were beaten, of spatters of dried blood on the walls of the White House, of the squeak of the beater's shoe soles on the concrete floor as he pivoted toward them, and the stomach-turning hiss of the whip just before it slashed their backs and their buttocks. The smells, the sounds, the expressions—*Boy, you're goin' down*—were all chillingly alike. And the same names were repeated time and again, Hatton, Tidwell, and sometimes Arthur G. Dozier, the former superintendent for whom the reform school was now named.

At the same time, the men had their own personal stories of horror. Michael and his terrible grief over the boy named Woody. Robert's assault by a faceless brute in a dark place they called the rape room. Willie Hayes and his daring escape from the rape room, when he yanked himself free from the guard's iron grasp and ran for his life, only to be recaptured and beaten nearly to death. Dick Colon's memory of seeing an African-American student tumbling in an industrial-sized dryer in the school laundry, and the shame he felt for not attempting to save the boy because he was too afraid. More than forty years later, he hadn't even told his wife about it.

Marbin Miller recognized a momentous story when she saw one, and this one had the potential to rock the state's juvenile justice system like no other—not the tragedy of Omar Paisley, or Martin Lee Anderson, or any of the dozens of other scandals she had uncovered in her years on the beat. In terms of sheer numbers, it was possible that literally thousands of young boys had been tortured in the name of the state of Florida—and that some may have died—while politicians and the people of Marianna looked the other way. Marbin Miller had documentation of the school's long, sordid history. She had the men who were willing to go on the record with their charges of abuse. But there was still one major hurdle she would have to clear before the story could move from her computer onto the *Herald's* front page. The abuses had taken place decades earlier. She needed a news hook, something that would make the story relevant to readers now.

Gus Barreiro grew increasingly worried with no answers from upstairs. Michael was calling him five and six times a day, hungry for information. What was taking so long? he would ask, pleadingly. How much longer would it take to get an answer? He sounded more desperate with every call. His fellow victims had put their trust in him, Michael said, and they were growing ever more dubious that he could accomplish what he had promised.

Barreiro told Michael to try to be patient, but he was jittery, too. He rarely slept through the night now. Every day he left his office wondering if the state would do what it usually did in the face of potential scandal: attempt to sweep it under the rug.

The word finally came down several weeks after the conversation with Frank Penela, the communications director. Barreiro was summoned to Penela's office. Several meetings had taken place with representatives from DJJ and the governor's office, Penela explained. After much consideration, they had decided the state would honor the wishes of the small group of men calling themselves the White House Boys, allowing them to return to the reform school in Marianna. Specifically, Michael and his band of reform school brothers would be permitted access to the punishment building they called the White House. The administration had chosen Barreiro to facilitate the men's visit.

Barreiro felt almost giddy as Penela outlined the agency's plan. If there could have been better news, he didn't know what it was. In all of his years of dealing with DJJ insiders, this was the first time he had seen them take a proactive rather than a defensive posture in response to a potential crisis. Barreiro had hedged when Penela mentioned that Carol Marbin Miller was poking around, asking if he, by any chance, knew how the *Miami Herald* had gotten wind of the story? Maybe one of the men had decided to contact the paper, Barreiro had responded, intentionally omitting the damning detail that he had paved the way for the exchange between Michael and the reporter.

Adding the *Miami Herald* to the mix had pushed the state into a corner, just as Barreiro intended. He decided to push it a step further by suggesting that DJJ turn the reporter's interest to their advantage by granting the *Herald* exclusivity and allowing Marbin Miller to accompany the men on their return to Marianna. That way, Barreiro suggested, not only would the agency ingratiate itself with the plucky reporter, but the coverage of the story would be limited to a single newspaper. Panela said he'd think about it.

Barreiro ran down the stairs to his office rather than waste time waiting for the elevator. He couldn't wait to tell Michael the news. When he picked up the telephone, he felt his heart skipping in his chest. He needed to move fast, before the powers that be had time to rethink their decision, and he was certain they would.

A tired-sounding Michael answered the phone.

"Hello, Michael? Michael! It's Gus! We're there, buddy. They just put me in charge of this thing. I have the green light to move forward. I can't even believe it myself. We don't have time to waste. When can you all be in Marianna?"

Michael walked the beach for a long time after he hung up the phone with Barreiro. It was morning in Costa Rica. The sun's rays warmed his pale skin and sand the color of gold cushioned his bare feet. There had been a time when the sensation of the sun on his face and the sand between his toes could coax him out of his darkest corners. But the gloom that was suffocating him showed no sign of surrender. He couldn't remember ever feeling so worn out, so fraught with feelings of self-pity and hopelessness. Once meticulous about his appearance, he had taken to wearing the same rumpled khaki shorts every day. His cropped beard had grown into a reckless tangle and daily bathing seemed to require more energy than he could muster.

Michael had smiled when Barreiro gave him the promising news from Tallahassee, and he had tried to sound enthusiastic when he thanked him. But summoning any more emotion than that seemed beyond his reach. All Michael could think about was Woody and how he had done nothing to try to save him.

And he feared that the only respite from the consuming sadness he felt was in a bottle.

He had survived Marianna once, barely. He wasn't at all sure he could do it again.

Seasoned journalists know that the best stories usually hinge on two basic components. Shoe-leather reporting and a little bit of luck had solved murders and ended presidencies. This story would not be the exception to the rule.

When Barreiro hung up from Michael, he called the *Miami Herald* with the stunning news that the state was prepared to acknowledge the White House Boys at a ceremony to be held on the grounds of the reform school.

That same week, Marbin Miller found Troy Tidwell's name in the Marianna phone book and cold-called the retired reform school superintendent.

She had a double hook.

CHAPTER NINETEEN

The date was set. A ceremony to acknowledge the White House Boys would be held on October 21, 2008, on the reform school grounds in Marianna, Barreiro reported to Marbin Miller. The White House Boys were invited to attend, along with a phalanx of official types, including Governor Charlie Crist and DJJ's top dog, Frank Peterman. The only media that would be notified would be the *Miami Herald*.

Barreiro knew that with each day closer to the event, the bureaucrats would become increasingly squeamish. The reservations began almost immediately after they had a date, with people from both DJJ and the governor's office calling to question the wisdom of a ceremony. Barreiro fielded their questions and concerns all day, every day. Wouldn't this mean that the state was acknowledging culpability in the tragedy of Marianna? they asked. What exactly would happen at the ceremony? Was there any possibility that the men would embarrass the state? Would they disparage the DJJ? Wasn't it best to keep the governor out of it? This hadn't happened on the Crist administration's watch. And what angle would Marbin Miller take? The idea had been that by hold-ing a ceremony, the state would seem benevolent in its treatment of the men, but how could they be assured that the reporter would see it that way? Couldn't this spiral into yet another black eye for DJJ? Aren't we opening up a can of worms?

Barreiro did his best to assuage the misgivings of his col-leagues. The bottom line was that it was too late for doubts and everyone knew it. The state had made the commitment to the men, and the state's most influential newspaper was aware of it. Backing out would be a public relations fiasco. Still, the admin-istration insisted on one final test before giving the ceremony their final blessing. They wanted Barreiro to set up a confer-ence call with Michael in Costa Rica so they could get a sense of him. If Michael passed the test, maybe the brass could rest.

Barreiro was blunt when he called Michael to tell him about the state's request for a teleconference.

"This is the deal," he said. "They're all having second thoughts. I'm getting it from all sides. DJJ. The governor's people. They're looking for a way out of this. This will be a make-or-break call."

The call was set up for the following week. Barreiro was joined in his office by Bonnie Rogers, the agency's chief of staff, Sama-dhi Jones from Penela's office, and Christie Daley from legislative affairs.

With Jennifer at his side, Michael introduced himself and launched into his story. He sounded articulate and sympathetic. Jennifer was glad the people in Tallahassee couldn't see his trem-bling hands. He and his White House brothers wanted nothing more than recognition from the state and a platform to tell their stories, he said, his voice strong and convincing. They had no intention of embarrassing the agency, or anyone in the current administration. They didn't want revenge, just the truth. When he talked about his reform school buddy, Woody, he broke down sobbing, but he quickly recovered.

Barreiro felt proud as he listened to Michael speak. He had become increasingly fond of him since their first conversation, several months earlier, and thought there was no more articulate or persuasive person to make the case to the higher-ups. The office in Tallahassee went still when Michael spoke of Woody and his fear that the youngster had never made it out of the White House alive. When Michael broke down, Barreiro told him afterward, there hadn't been a dry eye in the office.

The staff had been reassured by the phone call, just as Barreiro had hoped. They told Michael the agency was committed to do the right thing, and that they would honor the boys of Marianna with a plaque and a tree on the reform school grounds. They were working on getting Governor Crist and Secretary Peterman to the ceremony, they said. And when the time was right, Bonnie Roberts promised, they would tear the White House down.

Barreiro breathed a sign of relief when the call was over. Everything was going as planned.

So far.

CHAPTER TWENTY

R obert had been home from the summer festival tour for three days when Carol Marbin Miller called requesting a meeting with him. He had covered fifteen thousand miles from May through September and barely had time to catch his breath before he was on the road to Miami. With a five-hour highway drive ahead of him, he had plenty of free time to think, unlike the road tour, when his mind had been focused on the minutiae of his work. It had been good, the time away. The tour was grueling, too much for most men his age, but he had been thankful for the distraction from his memories of Marianna.

There had been moments, after wading into his reform school past, when Robert felt as if he might literally drown in his childhood recollections. Now, driving south on I-75 from Clearwater to Miami, he wondered how he could adequately convey to the reporter the effect that Marianna had had on his life. How could he explain to her that it wasn't so much the actual torture he had endured at the reform school that had killed something inside him, but the malice of a few sadistic men toward a lost, lonely boy? That defenseless boy had numbed himself to be able to survive the cruelty he endured there, and then he had buried that terrible chapter of his past in order to survive the rest of his life. Yet what kind of life had it been? he asked himself as he headed down the Florida coast. He had never been able to trust. Never been able to give or accept love. Never allowed himself to feel abandon with anyone. Never been able to hold a relationship together, not even with his own child.

Somewhere along the line, his mind snapped from the terrible sadness that languished so deep within him that he had forgotten why it was there. And then, a lifetime later, the memories surged over him like water from a burst dam, and he held his breath until he thought his lungs would explode. Miraculously, Robert thought, he had survived the torrent and, in a funny way, even felt cleansed by it. Whether he would ever be able to repair his broken spirit, he didn't know. But somehow, since he had begun to face that hellish stage from his tender years, his heart felt softer and the seething rage that had slowly eaten him his whole life seemed to have quieted some. Finally, the recurring nightmares—the one of the man sitting on the edge of his bed, and the one about confronting the monster in the pit—had ceased, at least for the time being. He could actually say the name "Tidwell" now without seizing with rage. He was thankful for that.

Yes, the break from the gloom had done him good, Robert thought. He had come a long way in the year since his past rose up and cornered him like a startled rattlesnake. He would tell the reporter that—how much it had helped to confront his childhood secret and be stronger for it. On the other hand, he felt guilty for having dropped everything in Michael's lap before he left on his annual summer excursion. His reform school comrade had appeared to be unbreakable during those early days of getting to know each other. In fact, Robert had found Michael's bravado intimidating.

But while Robert was on the road making a living, he learned Michael's veneer had shattered and he hadn't been able to piece himself back together. The hardened exterior had apparently been a cover for the fragile soul underneath. Now Michael seemed a pathetic figure, one minute shedding the bitter tears of the injured boy inside, the next minute trying to exert tightfisted control over anyone he perceived as challenging his self-imposed authority. Robert felt responsible for Michael's anguish. If it hadn't been for him, he thought, maybe Michael would have lived out his life without ever confronting his recollections from Marianna. Michael might still be living his enviable life, happily married to a beautiful, younger woman, writing and developing documentaries.

He doubted it, though.

The pain of Marianna was so acute that it transcended even the men who lived with it. The reform school had been a scourge on society. How many angry boys had left Marianna and ended up in prison because they sought their vengeance through crime? Robert wondered. How many men had cracked and couldn't be put back together? Ticking time bombs, still out there, threatening to explode? Long ago, a would-be robber in a dark parking lot had approached Robert and Robert beat the man with a tire iron, continuing to attack long after the man ceased to make noise. Sometimes he still felt as if he could kill someone if he were provoked.

By the time Robert reached Miami and the *Herald* offices, he was exhausted from his thoughts. The newsroom was impressive, he thought, a cavernous room with endless cubicles and people running back and forth with a sense of great urgency. He wasn't sure what to expect or what was expected of him. Carol Marbin Miller was just as he had imagined. She was bookish, with a kind of detachment. Dispassionate, Robert thought, sitting on a stool across from the reporter, that was the best word to describe her. Marbin Miller oozed competence and Robert felt comfortable in her presence. He thought she sounded like a therapist as she coolly explained what was about to take place.

Michael had been interviewed for the piece a few days earlier, Marbin Miller said. She had asked him the same questions she was about to ask Robert. Three other men had also agreed to go on the record, she said. Robert would be photographed, the reporter explained in her strong, steady voice, and then she would begin the interview. It would take the better part of the afternoon, she said. A videographer would be filming them for a Web presentation to accompany her story.

Robert suddenly realized the import of the meeting. If I'm sitting at the *Miami Herald* and they're videotaping me, he thought, and they're talking to the other men and doing the same with them, they're going to break the story. Michael had done his job well, Robert thought. He had done what neither Robert nor any of the other White House Boys had been able to do: convince someone in power that what happened in Marianna was iniquitous and that the sins of the state had to be aired.

Robert straightened his glasses and sat up on his stool. The videotape whirred and he began ticking off 108 years of disturbing historical facts from the Florida School for Boys. Marbin Miller listened patiently. Yes, she said, she knew about the shackling and the hogtying, about the fire, and the isolation cells. She knew about the occasional feeble attempts by politicians to get things changed at the reform school, and the testimony from experts before the Florida state legislature that went unheeded. She had done her homework, Marbin Miller said. It was Robert's personal experience she wanted to know. What had it been like to be taken to the White House? she asked. How badly had he been beaten? Had he felt fear and intimidation by the guards? What had it done to him, being there?

Robert had been stoic for the first part of the interview, but he grew flustered talking about his own terrible experience. His eyes widened and he looked like a frightened child as he spoke. "It was something you never get over," he said, his voice choking. "It will follow you for the rest of your life. It put anger in me that will never die. When you inflict that much pain and brutality on a child, they're traumatized for life. It's irreversible, and basically, what you're creating is a mini-monster." Robert broke down. His emotions were raw. What would he say to the men who did this to him, if they were there? the reporter asked. What would he say to Tidwell, who was still alive and living in Marianna?

Robert was stunned. "Tidwell?" he asked. "Tidwell is alive?"

Tidwell had been caught off guard by the reporter's call a few days earlier. When she told him she was writing a story about the reform school, he began telling her stories about the boys he had helped over the years. The one-armed man seemed to catch on when Marbin Miller asked about the type of punishment that was meted out when boys at the reform school misbehaved. "We would take them to a little building near the dining room and spank the boys there when we felt it was necessary," he had sputtered.

Robert took a breath and fought to control his rage. For months he had wondered if Tidwell or any of the other abusers might still be alive, and a few times he had promised himself that he would try to find out, but he had always been too afraid. What would he do if he ever came face-to-face with his abusers? Robert feared he might kill them.

What would he say to them if he had the opportunity?

"I would ask them what the *hell* were they thinking when they did this to me," he said, biting his quivering lip. "I'll tell you, it was just a very bad place to be."

While Robert reeled from the news that the man who had robbed him of his boyhood innocence, who had taught him just how cruel humanity could be, was still alive, the Marianna Rotary Club was honoring Troy Tidwell with the Paul Harris Fellow award for a lifetime of "Service above Self."

CHAPTER TWENTY-ONE

A week before the ceremony was scheduled to take place in Marianna, Barreiro called Michael with the news that neither Governor Charlie Crist nor Secretary Frank Peterman would be in attendance. He tried to prepare Michael for the worst. If for some reason Marbin Miller's story didn't run as scheduled on the coming Sunday, Barreiro said, there was a real chance the state would still try to back out.

Michael flew from Costa Rica to Miami that Saturday, October 18, 2008. He would wait to see if the story appeared in the *Miami Herald* the following morning, then rent a car and drive to Marianna for the Tuesday ceremony. His head was swimming with thoughts as he tossed and turned that night, all alone in a cramped hotel room, far from Jennifer and their new home in the Caribbean. What if the paper decided not to run the story at the last minute? he wondered. What if the reporter hadn't seen things his way? What if no one cared? Michael dreaded the thought of letting the other men down.

The mission to expose the reform school tragedy had been

fraught with roadblocks, and Michael had become increasingly unsteady with each one. The more he had begun to doubt himself and his ability to do for his persecuted former schoolmates what he had accomplished for the victims of Rosewood, the harder he tried to control everyone and everything around him—and the more ground he lost. His increasing rigidness and bullying as his insecurities grew hadn't boded well with Robert and his other White House cohorts, and he had begun to feel alienated from them. The relationship with Jennifer was slipping through his fingers, his documentary work had fallen away as he devoted more and more time to the White House mission, and his resolve not to drink had weakened to the point that he wasn't sure how much longer he could abstain. There wasn't a day he hadn't cursed the moment he sat down at his computer in Greenville and opened that e-mail from Robert.

The sun was barely visible on the horizon when Michael grabbed a copy of the Sunday *Miami Herald* from the box outside his hotel. He tucked it under his arm and rushed back to his room to read it.

OCTOBER 19, 2008

A PAINFUL REUNION AT SCHOOL OF HORROR
BY *Carol Marbin Miller*
MARIANNA—The Florida State Reform School—more dungeon than deliverance for much of its 108-year history—has kept chilling secrets hidden behind red-brick walls and a razor wire fence amid the gently rolling hills of rural North Florida.

The article went on to recount the school's sordid history and efforts over the years to reform the institution.

On Tuesday, about a half-dozen alumni will return to what is now called the Arthur G. Dozier School for Boys to confront the most painful chapter of their troubled lives.

The White House Boys, as a group of grown men now call themselves, kept one of the institution's most shameful secrets for half a century: what was done to them inside a squat, dark, cinder-block building called The White House.

Marbin Miller reported on the former students' claims of having been ferociously beaten in the White House and sexually abused in a so-called rape room.

State juvenile justice administrators, who have not denied the allegations, will dedicate a memorial to the suffering of The White House Boys—who found one another through the Internet—at a formal ceremony at the Marianna campus Tuesday.

They number in the hundreds, perhaps even thousands.

The story quoted eighty-four-year-old Troy Tidwell as saying that boys were disciplined at the school, but that the "spankings" were never so severe that they were seriously injured.

"We would take them to a little building near the dining room and spank the boys there when we felt it was necessary," Tidwell said.

"Some of the boys didn't need but the one spanking; they didn't want to go back."

As Michael read Marbin Miller's stirring prose, some of his misgiving began to melt away. The reporter got it, he thought as he devoured her words. This wasn't just the tale of a few old guys making fantastic claims. It was a thoroughly researched and sourced investigation by a journalist with unimpeachable credentials, in which the state had conceded transgressions. And one of main perpetrators was still alive and had talked. People couldn't help but pay attention.

The Herald story was the break that Michael had been waiting for, the chance for a public airing of the truth. He was politically savvy enough to know that it would trigger a wave of publicity and, as the story spread, more victims would come forward—men who had suffered in silence for too long, as he and Robert had, who might find some solace in the company of their reform school brothers. Somehow, he felt validated. Maybe he had done his job after all.

Michael finished reading and called Barreiro, who had also risen early to get the paper.

"Did you see it?" Michael asked.

"It's magnificent, Michael!" Barreiro said. Michael could hear the smile in his voice. "This is it, Michael!" Barreiro said. "This is what you've been working for. This is the bombshell."

The tremors would be felt all the way to Tallahassee.

Barreiro could hardly wait for Monday to gauge the reaction of his colleagues at DJJ. The place was buzzing when he got there. Carol Marbin Miller was feared by the agency and they had expected to be excoriated in the piece. The reaction to the story was mixed. Some felt that she had been too hard on DJJ, but others were grateful for what they saw as a hard-hitting but fair report. The agency had expected to take a hit, because the stories of abuse were just too terrible and the men in the story were sympathetic characters, but the administration was hoping that any public outrage would be tempered by the years that had passed since the abuses and the state's willingness to acknowledge the men so many years after the fact.

"This is a positive thing," Barreiro insisted, sensing the apprehension of higher-ups. "We did the right thing. These men deserve our apology. They deserve the truth."

All day, Barreiro fielded calls from agency insiders. Some expressed shock that such a vile thing happened to those poor boys on the state's watch. Others wondered why DJJ had waded into such muddied waters. Why hadn't the agency simply ignored the men's claims? "Why are we even going down this road?" one manager asked. "It happened years ago."

"Yes, it happened a long time ago," Barreiro responded. "But it happened."

By noon, Barreiro began hearing sighs of relief from upstairs that no one had called to follow up on the *Herald*'s story. It looked like the agency might slide under the national radar, and that was at least good news. If they could just get through Tuesday's ceremony relatively unscathed, the story and the men would hopefully fade away and DJJ could put this ugly chapter to bed. The brass held their collective breath.

Michael was driving on the Florida Turnpike, on the way from Miami to Marianna, on Monday afternoon when Barreiro called him to convey the agency's reaction to the Marbin Miller story. His bosses were holding up under the pressure, he said, but barely. No one had said anything about canceling the ceremony, but they were jumpy about possible fallout from the *Herald*'s story.

"They're not going to alert the media about tomorrow,"

Barreiro said. "They want to try to contain the story as much as they can."

Michael exploded. "Wait a minute, Gus," he said. "How can they control it? How can they keep the media away?"

"I'm telling you," Barreiro said, "they told me no open press conference. They don't want to invite any more scrutiny. They don't want a bunch of reporters and photographers there.

"But if they come to the gate," Barreiro added coyly, "I'll have to let them in."

The distance from Miami to Marianna is 550 miles. The road trip takes between eight and nine hours. Michael was on his cell phone the whole way, calling every major Florida newspaper and television station: "Hello, my name is Michael O'McCarthy and do I have a story for you. Did you by any chance read yesterday's *Miami Herald*? The story about the Florida School for Boys? If you didn't, you should. It's a blockbuster. I want to invite you to a ceremony tomorrow in Marianna . . ." As it turned out, Tuesday's daybook was full up at most of the newspapers and television stations he called. The 2008 presidential election would be held in two weeks, and Democratic candidate Barack Obama and his wife, Michelle, were campaigning in the state. Republican candidate John McCain had scheduled a press conference with Governor Charlie Crist in Tallahassee for Tuesday afternoon. As they were sure he knew, most of Michael's contacts politely explained, the news industry has far fewer resources than it once had, but they would see what they could do.

The biggest fish in the shrinking sea of journalism was the Associated Press, a worldwide news agency that gathered and shared news stories with most of the media outlets in the United

States and abroad. Michael called the AP bureau in Tallahassee and got a reporter named Brendan Farrington on the telephone. "You really need to read the *Miami Herald*'s story," he told the reporter. "Please, at least take a look at it before you decide not to come." Farrington promised he would.

Getting the AP there, now that would be a coup, Michael thought, as he headed north toward Marianna, trying not to think about how it would feel to return.

CHAPTER TWENTY-TWO

The journey to hell had begun a half-century earlier, with the winding driveway leading up to the reform school in Marianna. On the morning of Tuesday, October 21, 2008, Michael shuddered as the shiny black SUV maneuvered through the sprawling campus, beginning the long climb toward his past. He glanced at Barreiro, who smiled reassuringly from behind the steering wheel, then he turned toward Robert, who was seated behind him. Robert gazed out the car window, forty-five years in the past, a million miles away. Michael turned back and stared straight ahead, watching the driveway fall away behind him. The campus looked much as it had on May 14, 1958, when young Michael got his first look from the backseat of a sheriff's van, and even then he had a sense of foreboding. "You just knew you had found a new kind of hell," he had told the *Miami Herald*.

How did I get here? Michael wondered as the SUV weaved up the hill toward the cluster of buildings at the crest of the grassy campus. How had his life taken such a dramatic turn in so short a time? It had only been yesterday that he was wrapped in a warm relationship and working at a profession he loved. Cautionary memories of the drinking life, and the misery that his addiction wrought on his early existence, had kept him sober for twenty-two years. Only a year earlier, he had been the happiest and the most content he had ever been. At least he thought he was.

Then, the earth shook and he fell from that magnificently benign life into the chaotic abyss of his denied past. What was it all for? he wondered as the car edged closer to his desperate need to confront the heartbreak of Marianna. His marriage was crumbling, his career was in shambles, and he still couldn't shake the craving for a goddamn drink. What had he gained by giving in to the insistence of a lost boy's despair? What was the sense of being there? he thought, as the car came to a stop on the grass next to the two-story brick administration building.

"Here we are," Barreiro said, his solemn voice abruptly suspending Michael's thoughts.

"Looks the same," Robert said, dreamily, hiding the fact that he was overcome with the dread of being on the campus again.

The men got out of the car and joined the handful of other men who comprised the group that had come to be known as the White House Boys. It was the first time they had all been together.

Barreiro led the way to the White House, passing the wooden school building, the mess hall, and the old superintendent's office. He could see Robert's chest heave and fall as they got closer to the torture chamber. He placed his hand on Robert's back, gently leading him forward. Robert didn't need direction, he said. He knew the way.

"There it is," Michael said, as the squat, whitewashed building crept into view. "What do you know, the White House."

Robert thought he might be sick. The building looked exactly as it had a half-century ago, maybe a little worse for the wear, he stammered. He wondered to himself if the blood-spattered mattress was still inside. The fan? The leather and metal whip?

Rows of folding chairs faced a podium that stood on the grass at the front of the tiny building. The sky was crystal clear, and a black sheath covering a dedication plaque fluttered in the warm autumn breeze. Fifty or so people had gathered at the spot, many of them employees of the Department of Juvenile Justice, some uniformed officers who worked at the reform school. Most passed the White House every day without knowing its history, and Barreiro wanted them to hear what took place inside. A gaggle of reporters and photographers gathered nearby. Barreiro had left instructions at the guard gate that anyone from the press who showed up was to be allowed in. All of the guests were chattering cordially until the White House Boys sauntered into the picture. Then, there was silence.

Michael had never felt so exposed, so alone, walking toward the group of strangers milling about the place where he and so many others had nearly lost their lives. Jennifer wasn't there, and the other White House Boys were subdued by their own memories. An early clash of egos had created tension among the men, and Michael was angry at their seeming lack of gratitude for what he had accomplished. Now he looked at them as he saw himself: wounded boys who were too damaged to sustain love or trust, too fearful to drop their protective veneers long enough to forgive. He wished he could tell them that he was frightened and headed over the edge, certain he was about to lose everything that meant anything to him: his wife, his living, his sobriety. But he couldn't tell them. That would mean revealing his own vulnerability, his own damaged soul.

Carol Marbin Miller and her crew from the *Miami Herald* greeted Michael, and Brendan Farrington from the Associated Press, who had heeded Michael's urging to attend, introduced himself. The ceremony was about to begin, Barreiro said. Would everyone please take their seats? Michael felt like running. Then he remembered he had a plan. When the ceremony concluded, he would linger long enough to close the door to the White House, locking his memories inside. He would say good-bye to Woody, after he told him how sorry he was for not being able to save him. And he would pray to the God he had never believed in to help him forget again. After that, he would go home to try to pick up the pieces of his life.

Barreiro walked to the podium and scanned the faces in the crowd. He had hoped the governor, or at least Frank Peterman, the head of DJJ, would reconsider and show up at the ceremony. But neither was there and he was disappointed. The White House Boys took their seats in the front row of folding chairs. Barreiro thanked the people in the audience for attending and the agency for allowing the ceremony to take place. He spoke of the men's courage and their willingness to return to the school to face the worst period of their lives. Then he invited the men to speak, uncensored.

Robert walked slowly to the podium. He cleared his throat, looked out over the heads of the people seated in the audience and recalled what it was like to be a frightened thirteen-year-old whose only crime had been running away from an unhappy home, and being snatched from bed in the pitch dark because "I was on the entertainment list for the night," he said. "That's what it was." As the audience listened in disbelief, Robert painted a vivid picture of Tidwell, "a man with an iron grip" grabbing a sleepy boy, for no apparent reason, and dragging him off to a night of hell. "They were monsters," Robert said. "Oh my God, the things they did." He looked at Michael, whose face was stained with tears. His friend looked so tired, he thought, so frail and vulnerable—nothing like the strapping man he met at the beginning of this terrible journey.

Michael had prepared a speech in his hotel room the night before, but he never took it out of his jacket pocket. Even reading his own words seemed like too much of an effort now. "I cried into that pillow," he said, his voice cracking. "I screamed into that pillow and they continued to beat me . . . and beat me . . . and beat me . . . and beat me." Looking at Robert in the front row, staring up at him with wide eyes, Michael was reminded of a frightened child, one that he wanted to shelter and protect. In a strange way, Michael thought, he cared for Robert in a way that he had never cared for anyone. Their shared horror had bonded them like brothers.

"I love you, Bobby," Michael said to Robert as he took his seat again.

Barreiro looked around. Tears streamed down the cheeks of some of the uniformed employees. I hope that the next time they think about punishing a child, they remember this, he thought. I hope they see that they hold kids' futures in their hands.

No one would make the point better than Dick Colon, the Baltimore businessman who said he witnessed an African-American student locked in a tumbling clothes dryer when he was a student at Marianna. Leaning on a wooden cane, the frail sixty-six-year-old man seemed to lapse into his past as he described a beating in the White House. "Jesus, God, what's happening to me," he cried as he recalled the first few lashes. "There was a boom, and it just kept coming, and the pain elevated itself with each lick. Get ready for the next one. Get ready for the next one. Here it comes again. Boom! Gasping for air. Gasping for air. Get ready. Get ready. Another one is coming." The people in the audience watched in stunned silence, some with their mouths agape, as he appeared to relive the experience before their eyes. With a few heart-wrenching words, Colon had brought the White House alive. And for the briefest moment, Michael thought he heard Woody screaming again.

Barreiro returned to the podium with tears in his eyes. He had been profoundly moved by the White House Boys and proud for the privilege of helping them to share their stories with the public. How often did someone have the opportunity to help another person through such a significant passage in their lives? he thought, as he prepared to make his closing remarks. The emotions of the morning had been so sad, so raw, but somehow Barreiro felt this was a new beginning for each of the White House Boys. And how many others would benefit from their anguish? he wondered. How many kids would be saved for years to come because of their courage?

Shortly before the ceremony, Barreiro had been informed that the state was reneging on its promise to demolish the White House. The bosses in Tallahassee had decided that such a move came perilously close to admitting culpability in the horrors that had taken place inside the white stucco structure. Now, he made an executive decision to pretend he hadn't heard about the state's change of heart—a decision that would seal his fate at DJJ.

"We have a commitment to tear down this building," Barreiro said, to audible sighs from the audience. Until then, he said, all of the children who suffered would be remembered with a budding crepe myrtle tree, to be planted on the side of the building, and a bronze plaque that read, "In memory of the children who passed through these doors, we acknowledge their tribulations and offer our hope that they found some measure of peace."

There was one last wish to be granted, Barreiro announced, inviting the men to walk through the White House before it was officially sealed. Willie Hayes, the corrections officer from Alabama who escaped from a guard's grip on the way to the rape room, then suffered a beating that should have killed him, stopped short of the door leading inside. Hayes was the size of a professional football player. He wore a straw cowboy hat, and had worked in corrections his entire life. He had dealt with the meanest thugs in the Alabama prison system and he never laid a hand on one during his nineteen years as a guard. But he froze at the thought of entering the White House again. "I can't," Hayes said in his thick Southern accent. Barreiro looked into his eyes and saw, not a sixty-five-year-old man, but a boy riddled with fear. "I just can't go in," Hayes said, whimpering. "I'll help you," Barreiro said, gently taking the man's arm and leading him inside. "Just take your time."

Michael would later say that walking into the White House was like entering a time warp. The crumbling building looked much as it had in 1958 when he had been forced to stand with his face to the wall and listen to the torture of Woody, whose cries, he feared, had been the cries of death. For a moment, the men settled in the chamber where the beatings had taken place. The room was bare, but in his mind's eye, Michael could see the bed and whip as clearly as he had fifty years ago. Robert stood by quietly, gazing at the spot where the whip had been stored. "This was not a trip to the woodshed," he told Marbin Miller. "This was not spanking. This was not a whipping. It was a flogging. I never heard anybody scream out in pain like that, except for the movies."

"Pieces of my hind end ought to be on that wall somewhere over there, where I took over one hundred lashes," Hayes said, choking up. "It is my sincere prayer that these horrible atrocities never occur again to any child."

"There was blood splattered all over the walls," Michael said. "God, I've got to get out of here."

As the White House Boys and their guests filed out of the White House, they passed a spot where someone, long, long ago, had scratched the name "Abraham" into the concrete wall. Beneath the name was a bloody handprint and the words "19 times." "Jesus," one of the state officials murmured as she walked out of the dank building into the brilliant sunlight.

With a simple hour-long ceremony, the state had acknowledged the most tragic chapter in its long and shameful history of treating troubled children. It was a stunning admission for any government to make. For a moment afterward, the White House Boys stood together in a show of unity—some with their faces distorted in anger, some seemingly lost in their memories. Only Michael stood alone. When the others turned to walk away, he said his good-byes to Woody, then pulled the door to the White House closed.

Robert lagged behind as Michael and the others headed to the administration building for sodas and sandwiches after the ceremony. When the others walked toward the front of the building, Barreiro summoned Robert to the back. A few curious photographers followed.

At least a dozen times that morning, Robert had asked Barreiro if he had located the underground chamber that the boys at Marianna had called the rape room. Barreiro said he hadn't had any luck finding it, based on Robert's recollection of where it was. There was no underground room in the schoolhouse, Barreiro said. He had, however, found an underground room beneath the administration building and thought that might be the room, and that Robert's memory had been mixed up by time.

Robert's eyes narrowed and he slowly shook his head. "No, Gus," he said softly, but resolutely, "I don't think I would have gotten that wrong."

"Just let me show you what I found," Barreiro said.

Barreiro guided Robert and the others down a narrow flight of stairs leading to a long, underground corridor. Robert instinctively turned right when he reached the bottom of the stairs. In his memory, the door to the rape room had been at the bottom of the stairs to the right. Now he stood facing a blank wall.

"This way," Barreiro said, motioning Robert to walk left down the long hallway.

"I don't remember any of this," Robert said, following Barreiro.

Barreiro walked to the end of the corridor and turned right, into a room much larger than the one Robert remembered. Robert looked around. The room was as least twice the size of the rape room, he thought. It was empty and swept clean, and a lightbulb hung from a ceiling wire. Robert looked for the telltale sign, the one that would leave no doubt in his mind that this was the place. The rape room had an escape hatch that led to an underground tunnel that ran beneath the campus buildings. Wire mesh had covered the entrance to the tunnel. The walls in this room were solid concrete.

Sunlight spilled in through the narrow windows at the top of two walls of the room. The windows were just as he remembered them, long and narrow. Maybe Gus was right, Robert thought. Maybe the escape hatch had been bricked up long ago. Maybe this was the rape room and his memory of the old schoolhouse had been wrong.

Robert's memories of the actual assaults that took place in the rape room were full of holes. He was certain that Tidwell had dragged him there by the arm, and that another man had grabbed him at the bottom of the stairs. When he realized he wasn't in the White House, he became frantic. He thought they had brought him there to be killed. He remembered Tidwell pushing him down on the hard floor, and one of the men climbed on top of him, shoving a bony knee in his back. He felt as if his own bones were crushing under the weight and passed out. The next thing he remembered was seeing his cottage lights off in the distance. The lights were blurry, as if he were looking through a Vaseline-smeared lens. Many years later, a psychiatrist had suggested that perhaps Robert had been carried back from the rape room to his bed, and that the blurry lights were because he had been delirious. Yes, Robert had said. That made perfect sense. He didn't remember how he got into bed that night, but he did recall how terribly sore his chest was when he awoke the following morning.

"Can't this be it?" Barreiro asked, his voice full of urgency.

"Well, I guess it could be," Robert said, wanting to please and beginning to doubt himself.

Robert pretended to be satisfied and turned and walked back toward the steps. The others followed.

"How did it feel, going down there?" a photographer asked Robert when they reached the top. "Well," Robert said, talking about the time he was taken to the rape room as a boy, "when I went there, I knew I was going to someplace worse than the White House. I thought I was going to be killed."

"C'mon," Barreiro said, changing the subject. "Let's all go get something to eat."

Only Barreiro had seen Robert leave the reception a few minutes after they arrived there. He commandeered a golf cart and rode off after him. He found Robert standing in the cool grass in the front of the old schoolhouse.

"You still think that room's over there, don't you?" Barreiro asked.

"I could swear it was," Robert said. "My gut instinct tells me it's there, yes."

"Do you want me to take you around the building to settle your mind?" Gus asked. "We searched all over and there is no underground room over there."

"If it's not too much trouble, I'd like that, Gus," Robert replied.

With Robert on board, Gus drove the golf cart slowly around the building, just as he had a few weeks earlier when he went looking for the underground room. "Over there," Robert said, pointing at the back of the school. The cart lunged forward. "Stop right there!" Robert said. Barreiro watched as Robert jumped off the cart and walked straight to a small section of the foundation. He bent down and pushed away a patch of vegetation. "Here it is!" he cried. "Gus, I think I've found it!" Barreiro ran to Robert's side. He couldn't believe what he saw. There, obscured by weeds and overgrown grass, was a small opening, barely large enough for a person to fit through. You had to be on top of it to see it. The opening was set off by a row of tiny windows; the kind that Robert had described, the same as the ones in the underground room in the administration building. Below it was a narrow set of six stairs, leading down to a padlocked cage door. Robert dropped down and kicked at the door. He kicked and kicked until his leg burned, but it wouldn't budge. He climbed back up the steps and examined the windows. A couple of broken panes were covered with a heavy wire screening. The corner of one was loose enough for him to fit a finger and then a hand through. Bracing his legs against the foundation, Robert grabbed the corner of the screen and pulled it with all of his strength. It pulled out just enough for him to get his head through. That was all he needed.

The rape room was exactly as Robert remembered, small and damp. And there, on the opposite wall, was the escape hatch leading to the tunnel. "This is it," Robert said.

Barreiro was stunned. "Well, I'll be damned," he said.

A few moments passed as Robert stood silently in the doorway, remembering that night, so many years ago, when he had been trapped under the anonymous man, a young innocent, wondering what he had done that was bad enough to deserve such a terrible fate. If he had had a choice then, he thought he probably would have chosen death over what happened to him in that room. There had been so many nights after that when he wished he was dead. Finally, he knew why.

Robert turned to Barreiro, who was standing beside him.

"Thank you, Gus," he said in his soft voice, his eyes welling with tears.

There was one more stop to make before the White House Boys would call it a day. Barreiro led the men across the street from the reform school campus and down a narrow path to the clearing where thirty-one boys were buried beneath crosses welded from rusted galvanized steel pipe. On Barreiro's orders, Marbin Miller had been permitted to search the school's file and was able to determine that some of the graves held the remains of the boys who died in the 1914 fire, but that only accounted for six of the crosses. Who else was buried there? the men asked. "We don't know anything," the current superintendent, Mary Zahasky said. "This is a memorial?" Robert asked. "A pipe in the ground?"

Barreiro explained how he had discovered the graveyard a few weeks earlier, quite by mistake, and had questioned everyone he could think of who might have knowledge of who was buried there, but no one seemed to know much about it. He had heard the stories from people in town about boys being drowned in the river, and boys being killed and buried randomly in the surrounding fields, but no one had ever mentioned a cemetery.

The group stood quietly for a long while, everyone lost in their own thoughts. It was Michael who finally broke the silence.

"We have to know who's buried here," he said. "We can't rest until we know."

When Michael left the reform school that day, he realized that his work was far from over. He couldn't absolve himself of his memories of Marianna—he couldn't lock them inside the White House and walk away—because the memories were not his alone to forget.

He couldn't walk away, no matter the toll the mission might take.

CHAPTER TWENTY-THREE

Monica Adams thought she was dreaming. She had dozed off while watching the television news in her Tampa home and thought she heard someone talking about the Florida School for Boys.

"They say those beatings took place in this building, known as the White House."

Adams rose up in her bed. There, on the television screen, was an image of a graying man identified as "Robert Straley, former student." "Just looking at it gives you the creeps, because if you were going down there you were going to get the beating of your life," Straley said, standing in front of a small, white, one-story building identified as the White House.

"My God!" she cried. "Oh, Ellis! My God!"

Adams finished watching, then spent a sleepless night waiting for morning to come so she could begin trying to track down the man in the story. The first thing she did was call the news station to ask where to begin. They gave her Straley's e-mail address. She sat down at her computer and composed a message.

"Dear Mr. Straley, I have a story to tell you."

Four years earlier, Adams had lost her husband, Ellis, to a terrible death. A kind man who had never hurt anyone in his life, she said, Ellis committed a slow suicide. It was as if, during his last years, he had given up wanting to live.

Monica had run away from home when she was sixteen to be with Ellis. He was a meek young man, with red hair and freckles, and he treated her like a princess. By the time her parents finally found her, she had just gotten home from the hospital with their first child, a boy. She and Ellis were married for thirty-five years, and for thirty of those years she had never seen him drink anything stronger than coffee or iced tea. But five years before his death, Ellis had sunk into a murky depression. A doctor prescribed antidepressants but the medicine hadn't been strong enough to ease his terrible sadness and anxiety. Sometimes he awoke screaming in the night. He began chasing the pills with glasses of brandy.

Monica had watched helplessly as her husband's personality changed. He cried for no reason and he was often angry. He would lash out, then say he was so sorry. When he was drinking, he would ask, "Monica? Why am I doing this? I hate liquor." She could only say she wished she had an answer. Monica loved Ellis. Loved him like nobody else. He had never been very ambitious, never held a job for too long, and, God bless him, he never finished much of anything that he started. It had been Ellis who did most of the childrearing while she went to work to pay the bills. But he was devoted to her and the children and they adored him. To watch him deteriorate and not know why was devastating.

But one day, out of the blue, Ellis started telling Monica about Marianna. About how he'd been sent there when he was ten or eleven years old for skipping school, and how frightened he'd been. The details came in dribs and drabs at first, but after a while it was all he could talk about. He remembered a one-armed man, named Tidwell, and a couple of others whose name he couldn't quite recall and said they were sadistic and cruel. Once, he had been flogged so violently that they thought he was going to die. He remembered counting eighty-one licks before he lost consciousness, and he hadn't even misbehaved, he said.

It bothered Ellis to the bone, what went on at the reform school. He had told her, "Monica, there were kids there and then you never saw them again. They buried kids up there in those woods. Somebody needs to dig up those grounds. Those kids were there, and then they were gone." Ellis said he had wanted to tell his secrets about Marianna, but he was too afraid. And later he had buried his memories for many, many years, but for some reason they had come back to haunt him and he figured that meant he was supposed to tell somebody. He had told Monica most everything, she guessed. But that still hadn't been enough to pacify him. He would say he wanted those bastards to pay, he just didn't know how to go about it. Once, at two in the morning, he had gotten out of bed and called Marianna to see if the school still existed. When he found it did, it had sent him into an even deeper funk.

So before he died, Ellis sat down and wrote a four-page letter with his memories of Marianna. He told his family to keep the letter in a safe place and, should anyone ever have the courage to reveal the sins of the reform school, which he hadn't been able to do, he wanted them to have it—so that he could bear witness to what happened there, even after his death.

Monica Adams had included her telephone number in the

message to Robert. He was still trembling when he called her. They talked for a while, and then Monica offered to send Robert the letter her husband entrusted to her and her children. Ellis would have wanted that, she said. More than anything else, he had wanted the perpetrators of torture on the boys at Marianna to pay for what they did to him and the other children. When she saw Robert on the news, Monica said, she knew that she would finally be able to grant her husband's dying wish.

The envelope arrived the following week. Robert tore it open and started reading.

"I remember being taken from home at a very young age," Ellis Adams wrote in 2004, years before Robert's memories of Marianna bubbled up. "I didn't want to go to school. My mother raised six children on $81 a month. That paid our rent, food, clothing, etc. I didn't want to go to school because I didn't identify with the other kids. I was very embarrassed for not having simple necessities such as shoes, lunch, etc. It wasn't my mother's fault. She did everything she could on her own. I remember the truant officer coming to our house all the time. He would grab me in the back of the pants and pick me up off the ground. I would cry in desperation and my mother could only stand there in sadness and grief, because she was helpless and . . . couldn't do or say anything to stop them from taking me away. . . . I remember the sadness on my mother's face. Because she did the impossible! On 81 dollars a month from the state she tried very hard to feed us and clothes [*sic*] us. I don't ever remember seeing more than one pot on the stove and it always seemed to contain beans. . . . That's all we seemed to have to eat, beans and mustard and onion sandwiches. I guess we were grateful for having anything to eat at all."

THE BOYS OF THE DARK

Robert cried as he read. There was a sweetness and a sincerity to the man's words that deeply touched him.

Ellis Adams went on to talk about the jobs he and his brother scrounged to help buy food. At one point, he was only eight or nine at the time, he had his own shoeshine box and he would stay out after dark shining men's shoes. He and his brother Don "walked many miles, going wherever we could to make a little money," he wrote.

"I remember we used to climb into the dumpsters at cigar factories and collect cigars," he wrote. "They seemed to be perfectly good cigars, but they threw them away, because, I guess they didn't pass inspection or something. We would sell them for a penny apiece. Usually we would make enough money to buy a pack of hot dogs. . . . I thank God for these memories. We were poor. But we had something no one could take from us. An honest love for others."

Robert noticed that the man's handwriting seemed to change when he recounted his time in Marianna. His neat cursive turned almost frantic. "This was around 1961 or so," the dying man wrote. "I remember something terrible, very terrible! happened there! I was awakened late at night after everyone in the cottage was asleep. It was the most horrible night of my life. I can't forget that night. It has really become engraved in my mind. God, why was this happening to me? Lately I have become very angry and I am tortured with this memory. I was awakened by a man. He was very small and thin with black hair and a mustache. I remember wearing very thin pajamas—like you were in a hospital. I was taken to a building behind the kitchen building. This place was called the White House. There was one door in the front, facing I think east. It was a small building. I remember this big door opening with a key and this corridor very narrow. . . . I asked him why I was there but he didn't answer me. He was waiting for someone else to arrive. Right inside the door there was one, I think, bed. I sat there waiting and very scared. At first I thought they were going to just lock me up. . . . Two more men, a Mr. Tidwell and [another man] arrived. . . . I knew something horrible was going to happen to me. I was taken into a room and placed on a small bed, about 3 feet wide, maybe 5 or 6 feet long. The bed was near the floor and had a filthy mattress on it. I was told to hold onto the end of the bed and not move or cry out. And then I remember the sound of something cutting the air, followed by a pain I can't describe. The most horrible pain a human being can imagine. I would try to move to get up from the bed. God make them stop beating me! But they beat and beat me and beat me so bad . . . I can't write any more about this. God make them stop."

Ellis Adams continued his story on a separate sheet of paper. He even drew a diagram of the campus, with the square representing the White House drawn in thick, black ink. "I can never forget the pain and fright I felt," he wrote. "Today I really believe no one ever felt such pain, physical and mental pain. The smell of sweat and blood on the bed. The sound of the large fan that somewhat drowned out the screams. My only thought was God! Please make them stop beating me. God! Please stop this. Please!

"I get very angry when I think about what they did to the body of a 10 or 11 year old," he wrote. "They weren't sick. They enjoyed what they did—and I only wish I could kill those bastards."

There hadn't been a good reason for Ellis Adams to die, according to his wife. He didn't have cancer, or a bad heart, or incurable disease. He simply got more and more tired until he stopped eating and finally went to sleep.

Monica Adams told Robert there were a few things eating at her husband during those last sad years of his life. Twenty percent were the things that bother most people, the kinds of things you somehow get over. Eighty percent was Marianna.

Ellis Adams's voice from the grave would be just the beginning of an avalanche of stories from men who had once been too frightened, or too traumatized, to come forward. Men who suddenly felt emboldened by the courage of a small band of brothers who called themselves the White House Boys.

"I was at the 'Boys School' three weeks before I gave them the opportunity to straighten me out," a man named Michael Tucker wrote. "I had asked to work in the kitchen. My main job was cracking open cartons of eggs. It was also my job to watch the serving line until my shift was up—this was when your cottage came in for lunch. One of my friends asked me to bring some extra butter with me, when I came to the table. You were only allowed 2 patties. I reached into the bowl and grabbed 4 or 5 patties. As I turned to leave, Mr. Edenfield was coming through the kitchen door into the serving area. I dropped the butter on the counter. He asked me what I had in my hand. I said 'nothing.' There, stuck to my hand was a patty of butter. He took me into his office, wrote me up for lying and stealing, and made me sign it. The fear built up during the day as I finished the afternoon at school.

". . . Confusion mixed with fear as I realized someone was pulling me up from the bed. I was told to keep quiet as I was led from the dormitory to a waiting car. There was another boy from a different cottage in the car, but we didn't look at or talk to each other as they drove us to the 'White House.' Inside we were taken to a small room with a cot and told to sit. A stocky man with one arm asked us if we knew why we were there. Another taller heavyset man was in the small hallway behind him. He pointed at me and said, 'come with me,' as the one armed man told the other boy to wait there and don't move. The tall man took me by the arm and we followed the one armed man across the hall to another small room. There was a cot with a bare mattress. He held onto my arm and told me to lie on the bunk face down. If I screamed or tried to get up they would get some of the bigger boys to hold me down. (I was later to become one of those bigger boys.) He said the best thing to do was get a mouth full of a flat little pillow under my head and bite down. The one armed man was choosing a strap as I was being instructed.

"I don't know [what] I was expecting, but it had nothing to do with the pain that exploded in my head when the skin split across my buttocks, a force that drove my whole body down into the bunk. Somewhere between that first lick and 33 licks later (even when you don't keep count you know) shock set in and my mind took me somewhere else. As the one armed man put the strap back, the big man was pulling me up from the bunk by the arm and asking me 'Can you stand up?' I sat in a daze of fear and numb pain on the bunk, where I had traded places with another then had to listen to the sounds of his pain as their licks drown him into the bunk.

"That was the first of 3 times I held onto that bunk while they beat me and made me realize they could do that to me anytime they wanted to. I could do nothing about it.

"There was a young boy, 11 or 12. His name was Tucker. I didn't know his first name but it didn't matter. Our [common] name gave us a certain bond. When Tucker came through the food line I always gave him a little something extra. I always saw him smiling, looking up at me in anticipation. It always made me feel sad for him whenever I saw the raw area that covered his chin as far as he could lick with his tongue. He licked it constantly from a nervous habit. God only knows what happened to him to bring him to a place like this.

"One day, I was called to Mr. Edenfield's office and told along with another one of the bigger boys to go with that same large man who, two months earlier, had given my instructions on how to take my beating. As I walked out the back door and realized where we were going, the fear set in. The 'White House' sat just out back of the kitchen. There are things in life that are done to you that scar your soul. [Inside the White House] lying on that cot was a boy whose eyes were as red and raw from crying as was his chin from constant licking. I knelt at the head of that bed that day, as I was told, and I held his hands behind his back while the other boy held his feet. I had only thought I had felt all the pain that room had to give, but as Tucker stared into my eyes that day, struggling against my grip with all the strength in his little body, begging for his mama while they beat him with that strap, I realized I hadn't. My soul began to understand the real cruelty of mankind. The next day I saw Tucker shuffling through the food line looking at the floor and licking his chin. He never looked up at me again."

One of the few African-American men to come forward was a man named Willie Horne of Atlanta whose harrowing tale included a claim of murder in the White House.

"I was on what they called the colored side," Horne wrote. "When I first got there I was a cottage brother. My cottage brother was King of the Cottage, which meant you behaved real good and got extra privileges. One day I became King of the Cottage. We had a blue clipboard with disciplinary reports. If I saw guys doing wrong, I wrote them up.

"My cottage father was in the loft upstairs and it was my job to deliver the disciplinary reports to him at the end of the day. This one day, when I knocked on the door, the door opened and I could see the cottage father and another guy in there having sex. I knew the cottage father saw me, and closed the door and went back downstairs. I never said a word about it. But my cottage father said I raped a kid in our cottage who was gay, which of course wasn't true. When they came and got me, instead of taking me to the White House they took me to a barn by Robinson Cottage. There were two big oak trees out there, close together. They tied me by the arms to the trees. Then they got a couple of the strongest guys from the cottage and they took turns beating me. When they were done beating me, they carried me to the hole. They put me in a dark cell with no toilet, just a can for number 2 and urine. I was 11 years old and they kept me in there for a month.

"One particular night, there were two white boys and another black boy with me when we were taken to the White House. When we got there they were whipping this white boy. He couldn't hold on to the [bed] rail, so when he let loose he rolled over. Tidwell, Mitchell [the director of the black side] and another white superintendent were there. When this happened, they took me and the other black kid back to our cottage. We never got our beating because they wanted to get us out of there. When we were leaving, I heard them saying, 'He shoulda held on! He shoulda held on! He shouldn't have rolled over.'

"I'll tell you the truth, and I'm not proud of it, but that place put hate in me. My older brother and me were both at Marianna and there were times, even many years later, when we thought about going back there and killing those people."

CHAPTER TWENTY-FOUR

There were just too many stories. Too many ruptured lives to be mended by a crepe myrtle tree and a bronze plaque. Robert spent every day reading the e-mails that poured in, hundreds of stories of lives scarred by the turpitude of silence.

"I spent 10 months 6 days and one hour in the most child abusive place I've ever heard or thought about. The staff there was far worse than the beasts you read about in the Nazi concentration camps."

"I was hitting my kids. I had to walk away. Leave all my dreams, leave my wife, friends and family because I didn't trust my-self. I visited my two daughters after 15 years, once I felt like I was OK. They were very angry, like I used to be angry. They would not let me into their homes or introduce me to their children. I guess I don't blame them. But I DID leave before I hurt anyone."

"We were taken to the White House where R. W. Hatton beat us this time so badly I almost passed out from the pain. I could hear

the blood splattering inside my underwear with every hit. I have nightmares to this day about that beating."

"I was in such pain I could barely answer yes. He told me to get up and he would take me back to my cottage. As I got outside, Hatton and some other guy and Tidwell traded some funny story and then I was taken back."

"The legacy of abuse did not stop in 1967. It continues today, as I have to remember the multiple beatings my brothers and I had to endure from my own father. He strives to be a good man but has never been whole since the day he was left at the boys' home in Marianna."

"[My father] said that the cemetery you found won't be the only one."

"I often wonder about the other guys that were there, and I pray that they got over it. My memory of that place has haunted me for a long time."

"I spent nearly 4 years there, that really changed my life. I turned out to be a criminal all the way up until I was in my late forties, two terms in Florida Reform School, Marianna, four terms in Raiford, three in Federal Prison, all because of what happened when I was only 12 yrs old."

"Whenever a child is subjected to brutality as these men were, it is their sons and daughters that end up suffering from something that happened before they were born . . . a sad legacy of rage that can burn its way through generations."

"As my brother had confessed to me, he was afraid for his life and some boys he knew simply disappeared, not to be seen again."

Turning on his computer by nine, Robert worked every day until midnight, sometimes too weary to make it to his bed. He answered every e-mail and every letter and when there was a telephone number included, he called. Time and again, the person on the other end of the phone burst into tears when he identified himself. Robert had never felt so useful, or so helpless. Marianna's reach was stunning, he thought. The insidiousness of the place had spread like a tsunami breaking on shore, ravaging families for generations forward.

One of the most stirring stories to come out of the reform school was that of Ovell Smith Krell, who was eighty years old and still searching for answers to her brother's death. She was twelve when her brother Owen, two years older, was found dead after escaping from the Florida School for Boys in 1941. Ovell had grown up to marry and have children, and for twenty-three years she served on the Lakeland police force—one of Florida's first female police officers. Her life had been filled with God's blessings, but she would never feel whole, not knowing how Owen died.

George Owen Smith had the wanderlust, and his hometown of Auburnville, Florida, wasn't big or exciting enough to keep him around for very long. He was a mischievous boy, as is clear in one of the last photos of him alive. In it, Owen is making a face at the camera, pulling his mouth wide apart with his index fingers. Yes, he had a bit of the devil in him, Ovell admitted, the way so many boys his age did. He never said when the urge to roam struck. He'd just be gone, usually to his grandparents' place on Gasparilla Island, 150 miles south of Auburnville. Then a little time would pass and Owen would come whistling down the street, home with happy tales of fishing the Gulf with Grandpa.

But in the spring of 1940, Owen left and didn't come home anymore. Ovell's mother, Frances, was beside herself with worry. Finally, the family received word that Owen was in a lockup in Tavares, Florida. Seemed he and a nineteen-year-old companion he met in his travels had crashed a stolen car. Unbeknownst to his family, Owen was then given a hearing and sentenced to Marianna. He wrote home when he first got there, then no one heard from him again. A few months passed, and Ovell's mother wrote Millard Davidson, the reform school superintendent at the time. The family was notified that Owen had escaped and was picked up by the Polk County Sheriff's Office in Bartow, Florida. George Smith went there to retrieve his son, but was told that Owen had already been returned to Marianna.

Owen wrote home once more after that, to say that, yes, he had run away and when he got back to the campus, "I got what was coming to me." Later, his family would learn that he had been carried to the infirmary after his beating in the White House.

Krell's mother wrote the superintendent a second time that October asking after her boy, but she didn't hear back. Then, just before Christmas, she inquired again. This time, the superintendent responded with more troubling news. Ovell still had the letter. Dated January 1, 1941, on Florida School for Boys letterhead, the superintendent wrote:

> *Dear Mrs. Smith,*
>
> *This is to acknowledge receipt of your letter of recent date written with regard to your son George Owen, and to advise that so far we have been unable to get any information concerning his whereabouts. We will be glad to get in touch with you just as soon as we are*

able to locate George and in the meantime we will appreciate your
notifying us immediately if you receive any word concerning him.

Very sincerely yours,
Millard Davidson
Superintendent

Three weeks later, frantic that her son was still missing, Ovell's mother wrote the superintendent to inform him that she would be traveling to Marianna within the week to see about her lost boy. Before she could even make her travel plans, the local preacher visited to say that he had been contacted by his Marianna counterpart, the pastor from Superintendent Davidson's parish, and asked to deliver the news that Owen's decomposing body had been found under the porch of a home in Marianna. Owen had apparently climbed under the porch after he ran away and either succumbed to the elements or starved to death.

Owen's distraught parents asked the local minister to contact the reform school and tell the superintendent they would be there to retrieve Owen's body the next day. When they arrived, however, they were escorted through the woods to a small clearing with unmarked graves and told that the spot with freshly turned dirt was where Owen's remains had been buried that very afternoon. The family tried to get answers that day, but "no one would talk to us about it," Ovell recalled. "No one would talk to us about how a healthy fourteen-year-old boy could climb under a porch and stay there until he died. It was like a shroud of secrecy in the whole town of Marianna."

No one, that is, except another boy from the Florida School for Boys.

Ovell remembered the boy telling them that he and Owen

escaped that night. They were headed toward town when they saw lights behind them and knew they had been discovered. The boy walked toward the lights to give himself up, but Owen took off across an open field. The last thing the captured boy heard before he was led back to the reform school was the blast of the guards' guns. He never saw Owen after that.

Nearly seventy years later, Krell was still looking for answers to the questions she had asked as a twelve-year-old innocent whose brother's early death just didn't make sense. How had Owen died? Had the guards killed him, like the boy said? Had he been caught and dragged back to the school and killed? Owen had been missing since September. If his body had been underneath the porch for that long, wouldn't someone have smelled it? As a police officer, Ovell had smelled death and it was not something you could ignore. Ovell believed she knew the answer to her brother's death. She didn't know if he died from a bullet or a beating, but she and her family had always believed that the staff at the Florida School for Boys was responsible for his death—that they killed Owen and then covered it up.

Ovell had kept another letter from that terrible time in her family's life. A letter from the reform school superintendent's preacher, V. G. Lowery, of St. Luke's Episcopal Church in Marianna, Superintendent Davidson's pastor. It had arrived at their home in Auburndale about the same time they returned from Marianna.

My dear Mrs. Smith,

I am anxious to send you this word of assurance that Mr. Millard Davidson did all in his power to provide a suitable and Christian burial for your son George. Mr. Davidson and all those in authority at the Florida School for Boys feel this most unfortunate happening very deeply, and it never would have occurred had it been in their power to prevent it.

Frances Smith took to her bed and stayed there every day for forty years. She would only leave her room in the evenings, to sit on the porch and listen for her son to come whistling home.

The cause of George Owen Smith's death was never officially determined.

By early December, Robert and Michael and the small cadre of men who had come to be known as the White House Boys determined that they needed much more than a ceremony to feel whole.

For the sake of Ovell Smith Krell and all the other victims like her, they needed answers.

CHAPTER TWENTY-FIVE

On Monday, December 7, 2008, the White House Boys held a press conference on the steps of the United States Federal Building in Tallahassee to demand a formal investigation of the unnamed graves at the Florida School for Boys.

Reporters poised their pens and video cameras whirred as Michael began reading from a prepared statement.

"Today, the White House Boys Survivors Organization formally calls upon the United States Department of Justice, Cold Case Criminal Division, Civil Rights Section, to begin a formal investigation into the identities of those human remains buried in a mass grave of what was called 'the colored boys side' of the then Florida School for Boys at Marianna, Florida.

"Given the long history of beatings, torture and rape and racism at that institution, we believe that the cause of death may have been 'foul play' committed in, but not limited to, that which has now been acknowledged to have taken place in the 'White House.'"

. . . Thus, we call upon the Department of Justice, Cold Case

Criminal Division, Civil Rights Section and the Attorney General to begin a formal investigation of these deaths that we believe may have been caused by officials of the Florida School for Boys while acting 'under the color of state law.'"

It was a bold move by a group of men whom the state had hoped would disappear with the planting of a tree—a burgeoning group that would not be bullied into submission by the state of Florida again. The White House Boys were serving notice: They would not rest until justice was served. Justice for the boy named Blackie, who had worked alongside Dutch Rowe in the carpentry shop and, as Dutch had told it, was murdered by guards who learned he was planning to escape. For the boy Willie Horne claimed lost his life because he moved the wrong way during a beating. For George Owen Smith, the boy with the itchy feet, whose body was hastily buried in the school graveyard before his parents could get there, and whose sister was still seeking the cause of his death nearly seventy years later. The White House Boys would not rest until they did everything in their power to see to it that those boys and all of the victims of the Florida School for Boys had not suffered and died in vain, and that the sins of Marianna would never happen again.

"Thus, we officially and respectively ask that Governor Charlie Crist show mercy for the victims of the pain and suffering caused at the Florida School for Boys by employees of the State of Florida; realize the pain of those who were voiceless and without rights during the time of Florida's participation in segregation; even more so that he understand that these were children who had literally no standing in law. We ask that he immediately respond to our call for justice and join with us and the Department of Justice in their investigation and lend all possible assistance.

"We ask that Governor Crist order an independent forensic investigation of these deaths and other criminal acts committed by officials under the color of state law upon the persons that were held in the Florida School for Boys at Marianna.

"Fearing that time and age may prevent the presence of witnesses or destroy evidence, we, the members of White House Boys Survivors Organization, being citizens of the United States, do notify the highest office of law enforcement in the United States and that of the State of Florida of the suspected crime of murder.

"Further, we request that the investigation include all other crimes by state officials acting under the color of state law, including but not limited to, slave labor of minors in violation of the federal and state child labor laws, sexual crimes against minors including aggravated rape of minors, sex trafficking of minors, kidnapping and attempted kidnapping of minors for the purpose of sexual assault and trafficking, and torture of minors by employees for the State of Florida."

The press conference concluded with the group announcing that they would file a claims bill with the state of Florida—as had been done with the victims of the Rosewood case—on behalf of all the victims of the Florida School for Boys "to make them and their families whole."

It was a brave, impassioned plea, but also a desperate measure. If the group's message fell on deaf ears, it could mean a blow not just to Michael and Robert, but to all the White House Boys who longed to have their voices heard. Would Crist rise to the occasion, or would he overlook their appeal the same way he had overlooked the press conference at the School for Boys two months prior?

They didn't have to wait long to find out.

Michael was in his hotel room in Tallahassee the next morning, packing to go home to Costa Rica, when a reporter called him with the news. It was staggering.

Governor Charlie Crist had gotten their message.

By way of a letter to Commissioner Gerald Bailey, which had just been released to the press, the governor was asking the Florida Department of Law Enforcement to begin a formal investigation of the Florida School for Boys.

It was a moment Michael had only imagined, a validation of all his efforts and Robert's over the preceding years. In a few simple paragraphs, Governor Crist paved the way for a full-scale investigation, and gave Michael and Robert a chance to see redressed the torment that had been inflicted upon themselves and countless others. It was the end of a long struggle, and the beginning of the next chapter in their efforts: a chance for the White House Boys to see their wounds finally healed.

"The White House Boys Survivors Organization has brought to my attention the horrible plight suffered by children who attended the Dozier School for Boys in Marianna, dating back to the early 1900s," Crist wrote in the letter dated December 9, 2008.

"In the area surrounding the school there are 32 unidentified graves, marked only by white metal crosses. Questions remain unanswered as to the identity of the deceased and the origin of these graves.

"I request that the Florida Department of Law Enforcement investigate this serious matter. I have asked the Department of Juvenile Justice to provide any assistance that is required. The review should include an investigation into the location of the graves, and what entity owned or operated that property at the time the graves were placed. Please review all available resources and make every reasonable effort to determine the identities of these remains. During the course of the investigation, please determine whether any crimes were committed, and if at all possible, the perpetrators of these crimes."

Michael hung up the phone and sat down on the bed. He had accomplished what he had set out to do. He had done all he could for the suffering children of Marianna.

Now he needed to try to heal the injured boy who lived inside of him.

CHAPTER TWENTY-SIX

Did I dream this belief?
Or did I believe this dream?
  —From the song "I Grieve"

When Michael returned home from Marianna he found Jennifer sitting at the table outside their home. A cluster of candles flickered in the darkness.

"Sit down," she said.

Michael took a seat next to his young wife. She took his hands and he could see that she had been crying. Two notecards lay on the table in front of them.

"One is yours," Jennifer said.

Michael took a card and turned it over. Written in Jennifer's neat cursive was the word "Childhood." She picked up the matching card and placed it on the flame from the candles, then invited Michael to do the same with his.

Michael sat in silence for what seemed like a long while. Then he took his card and gently placed it on the flame.

Slowly, the paper caught fire, its edges curling into a bright orange glow.

They watched until all that remained was ashes.

EPILOGUE

MICHAEL O'MCCARTHY died of a heart attack after undergoing routine back surgery in Costa Rica on April 3, 2010. He was sixty-seven. All who knew him were stunned by his death. Only days earlier, he had written a call to arms to his White House brothers after the state announced that it would not prosecute their alleged abusers because of a lack of physical evidence. "By now, you must know that I am an eternal optimist," Michael wrote to Robert and the others at the end of March. "I never quit. I always believe that when I try, there is a way, and now we are faced with what to do about that fucking place, and the state of Florida, one more time. I am not giving up."

With his sudden death, victims of the Florida School for Boys lost one of their greatest champions. "Michael had the heart of a lion, the spirit of a warrior, and the courage to make a stand, regardless of personal sacrifice, for the needs of those who had no voice or hope," Robert said. "Our voice was his voice, and he used it fearlessly."

In a story in *The Miami Herald,* Carol Marbin Miller wrote that Michael's life "had changed dramatically" after he took up the fight for the White House Boys.

Gus Barreiro told the *Herald* that he believes the fight cost Michael his life. "It killed him, and it drained him," Barreiro said. "He was consumed by it."

Indeed, in the last months of his life, Michael had taken up drinking again, and Jennifer and her son had moved back to the United States.

Jennifer returned to Costa Rica to claim Michael's body. "When I first saw him, it was very difficult," she said. "I went there believing that I had so much to say, but in the end, all I wanted to do was to tell him how much he is loved and how he can finally let go, that I forgave him."

Although the crusade of Michael's life may well have contributed to his death, it will not end now that he is gone.

Said Robert, "He is now that soft whisper, an invisible hand on my shoulder as we journey on."

ROBERT STRALEY gave up his life on the road selling trinkets. He has spent the last year trying to atone for misdeeds he attributes to the damage done him at the reform school. Telling his story has set him free from his tortured past, he says. His former wife read about the White House Boys in the newspaper and contacted Robert after not speaking to him for eighteen years. She had known nothing of his experience at the Florida School for Boys. The two have since reconnected and are in the process of working out their differences.

He no longer has nightmares about Marianna.

GUS BARREIRO was fired from his job at Florida's Department of Juvenile Justice in January 2009. The state claimed that an internal audit of his computer revealed sexually explicit photographs of women downloaded from the Internet. Barreiro denied that he viewed pornography and said up to seven coworkers knew his password. He claims he was set up by the state because of his role in exposing the atrocities at Florida School for Boys. He says he plans to run for a political office again.

THE FLORIDA DEPARTMENT OF LAW ENFORCEMENT issued a summary of the first phase of the investigation on May 14, 2009. The report states: "It was determined that neither the school nor its staff made any attempt to conceal any student deaths. Furthermore, no evidence or information was discovered which indicated that any staff member was responsible for any student deaths at the school."

The conclusions were based solely on records of student deaths kept by the school.

"It has been 56 years since the last known burial at the School's Cemetery," the report states. "In the time span since, there is no known documentation or personal knowledge as to the precise location of each grave, or more importantly, which grave belongs to which student, staff member, or even school pets.

"There is also no known documentation that the graves ever had markers that would have individually identified the deceased.

"Although it is possible to exhume the deceased in an attempt to confirm identity, without knowing the precise location of each grave, it would not be possible to exhume any one individual gravesite. Attempts to exhume an individual's gravesite would likely result in the destruction of the entire cemetery and the des-ecration of its most innocent remains. Additionally, the physical condition of the remains would make specific identification un-likely. There is no known evidence that any of the deceased were embalmed or buried in sealed or structurally sound caskets. The possibility of confirming identification based on DNA may be dif-ficult due to these burial conditions alongside other contributing factors including advanced decomposition, environmental ele-ments, passage of time and a deficiency of suitable familial candi-dates for comparison.

"Exhumation in the State of Florida requires a court order is-sued by a Judge with jurisdiction for the area of the gravesites. Although the requirements for the issuance of a court order are not specifically enumerated in state statute, there are elements common to previously issued exhumation orders. An affidavit requesting the exhumation order would include the following elements; a compelling legal reason for exhumation (usually prob-able cause that the deceased died as a result of criminal conduct and that an examination of their remains would reveal evidence to further prosecution of the criminal case), a reasonable likeli-hood that an autopsy will disclose relevant information essential to the investigation, and the opinion of a forensic expert that there is a reasonable likelihood of relevant and essential evidence being obtained.

"In addition to the referenced criminal, legal, and forensic con-cerns, previously issued exhumation orders have acknowledged and addressed conflicts raised by religious beliefs and the feelings of family members and friends as it relates to the exhumation process.

"It does not appear that the results of the investigation support the issuance of any exhumation orders. The investigation did not reveal evidence to suggest that any of the deceased died as a result of criminal conduct which had not been previously investigated. Therefore it is highly unlikely that an autopsy would reveal any information relevant to the investigation."

The report concludes:

> • The entities that operated the School during the time the graves were placed (1914–1952) were: Governor Appointed Commissioners and The Board of Commissioners of State Institutions.
>
> • Thirty-one (31) individuals purportedly buried in the School's Cemetery have been identified. Of those 31 individuals identified:
>
> ▪ Five (5) individuals, between 1919 and 1925, had no listed cause of death and their only notation was that they were buried in the cemetery.
>
> ▪ Twenty-four (24) individuals died as a result of illness or accident.
>
> ▪ One (1) death was a homicide by identified assailants.
>
> ▪ One (1) cause of death was undetermined (1941 Coroners Inquest) due to advanced decomposition.

"In all cases, the deceased were accounted for in official documentation. There is no evidence to suggest that the School or its staff made any attempts to conceal and/or contributed to the deaths of these individuals. There is no evidence to support that an unidentified perpetrator exists or existed that was responsible for any of these individuals' deaths.

"Therefore, from witness testimonies, records that were examined and all information currently available, FDLE determined that there was no indication of a criminal predicate to warrant further investigation into this matter. The investigation pertaining to the School's Cemetery will be closed due to lack of evidence as defined by Florida Statutes.

"A separate report will be prepared regarding the allegations surrounding the abuse of the students."

At a press conference to announce the conclusions, investigators admitted they relied sometimes exclusively on interviews with former staffers and records kept by the school. They interviewed Troy Tidwell, but not Ovell Smith Krell, whose brother is supposedly in one of those graves and whose cause of death was never determined.

An editorial on May 24, 2009, in the influential *St. Petersburg Times,* which covered the story extensively, called the investigation a whitewash and an "utter disappointment."

"It was a band of former residents from fifty years ago, now calling themselves 'the White House Boys' who pressed (Gov.) Crist to act in December. . . . Grown men, many of whom have struggled to build a life in the wake of Dozier, told reporters life at the school could include strap whippings . . . that left blood on the walls and sexual abuse in an underground 'rape room.' Their accounts included witnessing boys trapped inside running clothes dryers, orders to dig child-size graves and friends who disappeared," the *Times* editorial said.

But rather than build on the testimony of alleged victims, the editorial pointed out, the FDLE relied instead on school records and old newspaper stories "which the agency conceded were incomplete and deteriorated" for its initial findings.

"It appears little weight was given to the fact that the official records would have been maintained by the alleged torturers themselves," the editorial said. "FDLE's first report suggests that the state needs to dig harder to uncover the truth."

Eight months after the state's report, on January 19, 2010, attorneys for the White House Boys wrote FDLE's commissioner, Gerald Bailey, offering their clients for questioning:

"Our purpose in making contact is motivated by several facts," Greg Hoag of the Masterson Law Group wrote. "First and foremost, it is to assist in and expedite the investigation which has been ongoing for over a year. Troy Tidwell, one of the individuals who our clients have indicated inflicted the physical and sexual abuse, is still alive. . . . Our clients are anxious to have the truth about the abuse officially acknowledged and appropriate action taken against those responsible.

"Another very important consideration," Hoag wrote, "relates to the reports of continued acts of abuse and mistreatment of boys at [the reform school] in Marianna."

Indeed, Marianna failed its 2009 evaluation, in which the state conceded that many of the same problems that the White House Boys exposed were still going on at the reform school fifty years later. Boys at the school reported they were fearful of the guards and some said they had been restrained, threatened, or struck. Fallout from the evaluation was strident and swift. Crist was quoted in the local newspapers as saying the failure was "inexcusable" and that the reform school should either clean up its act or be shut down. Reform school superintendent Mary Zahasky resigned under pressure, saying the department "has lost faith in me."

But officials and residents of Jackson County fought back, saying that closing Marianna would result in job losses. A new superintendent who promised change was hired in January 2010, and, in February, Florida's Lieutenant Governor, Billy

Kottkamp, paid a visit to the campus and said he was satisfied with what he saw.

"You get a sense from the people that work here that they are dedicated to their mission," he told the local ABC news affiliate at the end of his short tour.

THE WHITE HOUSE BOYS has grown from the original group of four to more than five hundred men who have joined in a class action lawsuit. The suit specifically names Troy Tidwell and charges him and other personnel at the school with disciplining boys "in an outrageous physically and psychologically abusive manner."

The suit charges that "While waiting for their beatings, the boys could hear the blood-curdling screams from other boys being beaten, which intensified the psychological trauma associated with the discipline."

On one occasion, it states, "after the blood curdling screams of a boy stopped, one of the state employees was heard to state 'I think he is dead' and the boys waiting in line for their beatings were discharged to return to their cottages without a beating. Plaintiffs believe that more than one child was killed by the Florida State employees by beatings or other means of torture.

"On another occasion, a child was placed in an industrial-sized clothes dryer which killed him. . . . On other occasions, some boys were sexually assaulted by State of Florida employees who worked at the Reform School for Boys."

TROY TIDWELL was deposed in his attorney's office in Marianna on May 21, 2009. Dressed in a blue sports coat over a burgundy-colored shirt with a matching pocket handkerchief, the eighty-four-year-old Tidwell seemed remarkably spry for his age, although he is a little hard of hearing. Sometimes feisty, almost aggressive, sometimes matter of fact, he said he spanked boys but never beat them. He admitted using a leather strap, but never more than ten times on a child, and never hard enough to make anyone bleed. There was nothing illegal about it, he said. The punishment was state-sanctioned. They called it Final Disciplinary Action.

Was the discipline he gave the boys at the reform school any different from the discipline he meted out to his own children? Tidwell was asked by Tom Masterson, the attorney in the civil case.

"No," Tidwell said.

Did the boys ever cry out when he beat them? Masterson wondered.

"No," Tidwell said.

Ever have other students hold down the children he was spanking? the lawyer asked.

"Yes, well, I was involved with the director, you know, having some boys from the kitchen to hold the boy down that kind of resisted, you know, the spanking, you know. . . . You always had to get the kitchen director to let us have two or three of the boys to hold the boy down to get a spanking," Tidwell said.

Two or three boys to help hold a boy down? Masterson asked.

"Well, it would be a big boy of course to hold them down like that," Tidwell answered.

How many boys did he figure he spanked over the years?

"I don't know," Tidwell said. "I can't say how many. I just never have even given that a thought, you know, to how many I spanked."

What did he think the spankings accomplish?

"One of the main reasons is control," Tidwell answered.

How did spanking the boys give you control? the lawyer asked.

"Well, if you got a kid that's misbehaving and he gets a spanking, sometimes it's one time, sometimes it's more than one time, I don't know if the spanking is the answer but I know the boys behaved better when that was going on than what they did afterwards," Tidwell said.

Did he think the spankings were effective because the boys were fearful of him? Masterson asked Tidwell.

"I don't think they were fearful of me," Tidwell replied.

Were they fearful of the spankings? the lawyer asked.

"I would think so," he said.

Did he ever consider that spanking children with a leather strap might be excessive punishment?

"I never did think nothing about that, because that was the rule when I went to work there, and I don't know how many years ahead of that it was enforced," Tidwell said.

"When you first arrived [at the reform school] they were using a wooden paddle?" the lawyer asked.

"Yeah," Tidwell said.

"And then they switched to the leather strap, and then for the next 30 or 40 years they continued to use the same leather strap until the late 60s?" Masterson asked.

"Until they stopped," Tidwell responded.

"Were you there when they decided there would be no more spankings?" the lawyer asked.

"Yes," Tidwell said.

"How did you find out? Masterson asked.

"Just talking to people," Tidwell said.

"You don't remember why they said they would no longer permit spankings?"

"No. Now, our superintendent, you know, he—of course, he

and the director—I mean, they were always having their meetings and I didn't attend any meeting that was discussed."

"Well," said Masterson, "it would seem to me that if you had been in a culture that was permitting spankings for 30, 40 years and suddenly they stopped, didn't you say, 'Why aren't we doing this any more?'"

"I didn't care nothing about it," Tidwell said. "The only thing I knew was the rule was made in Tallahassee and handed down to the boys' school. And I didn't have to ask no question like that."

Tidwell lives in a little white house in Marianna, protected from prying eyes by family members and neighbors.

The community has begun a Troy Tidwell Defense Fund.

THE FLORIDA LEGISLATURE has before it a claims bill filed in August of 2009 by Florida senator Arthenia Joyner on behalf of the victims of the Florida School for Boys. The bill states that the boys at Marianna suffered "physical and psychological abuse" that "included beatings in which the boys were forced to lie face down on a blood-stained cot" and were "struck repeatedly with a leather razor strap." Boys as young as ten were "severely beaten, requiring the pieces of their cotton underwear be extracted from the boys' flesh," the bill reads. Other victims "needed medical attention," and others "were placed in solitary confinement for as many as 30 days" in an eight-foot windowless cell with a bunk and a bucket. The bill seeks unspecified compensation for the victims.

The bill is being held in abeyance pending the outcome of the lawsuit.

THE WHITE HOUSE has been officially sealed.

CPSIA information can be obtained
at www.ICGtesting.com
Printed in the USA
BVHW070034271222
654949BV00047B/923